Argumentation: The Study of Effective Reasoning, 2nd Edition

Part I

Professor David Zarefsky

THE TEACHING COMPANY ®

PUBLISHED BY:

THE TEACHING COMPANY
4151 Lafayette Center Drive, Suite 100
Chantilly, Virginia 20151-1232
1-800-TEACH-12
Fax—703-378-3819
www.teach12.com

ISBN 1-59803-118-X

David Zarefsky, Ph.D.

Professor of Argumentation and Debate, Professor of Communication Studies, Northwestern University

David Zarefsky received his B.S. (with highest distinction) from Northwestern University and earned his master's and doctoral degrees also from Northwestern. He has taught at Northwestern for more than 30 years. From 1988 through 2000, he was dean of the School of Speech. Currently, he is Owen L. Coon Professor of Argumentation and Debate and Professor of Communication Studies.

Dr. Zarefsky has served as president of the National Communication Association (NCA), one of the nation's oldest and largest professional organizations for scholars, teachers, and practitioners in communication and performance studies. He also has been president of the Rhetoric Society of America (RSA), an interdisciplinary society of scholars interested in studying public discourse. He has held a number of other leadership positions in NCA and other professional associations and is a former editor of the journal *Argumentation and Advocacy*.

A prolific writer, Dr. Zarefsky has written five books and edited three more and has an impressive list of scholarly articles and reviews to his credit. He received the 1986 NCA Winans-Wichelns Award for Distinguished Scholarship in Rhetoric and Public Address for his book *President Johnson's War on Poverty: Rhetoric and History*. He won the same award in 1991 for *Lincoln, Douglas, and Slavery: In the Crucible of Public Debate*. He is one of only three people to have received this prestigious award twice.

A nationally recognized authority on rhetoric, argumentation, and forensics, Dr. Zarefsky maintains a busy schedule as a member of external review committees for departments of communication studies, as well as of speech communication, at various universities. At Northwestern, Dr. Zarefsky teaches undergraduate and graduate courses in the history of American public discourse, argumentation theory and practice, and rhetorical analysis and criticism. He has been elected to Northwestern University's Associated Student Government Honor Roll for Teaching on 13 occasions.

Table of Contents
Argumentation: The Study of
Effective Reasoning, 2ⁿᵈ Edition
Part I

Argumentation: The Study of Effective Reasoning, 2nd Edition

Scope:

This series of 24 lectures examines a common but understudied aspect of human communication: argumentation. Far from the stereotypes of contentiousness or quarrelsomeness, argumentation is the study of reasons given by people to justify their acts or beliefs and to influence the thought or action of others. It is concerned with communication that seeks to persuade others through reasoned judgment. The course is introductory in that it does not presume any prior study of argumentation. Because all of us practice argumentation, however, the course is also sophisticated in that it offers a systematic analysis, a precise vocabulary, and a philosophical foundation for what all too often is an activity that we conduct intuitively and unconsciously.

The first four lectures provide the necessary intellectual background. Lecture One defines argumentation and situates it among a family of terms: *rhetoric, logic,* and *dialectic.* Unfortunately, these terms either have acquired negative stereotypes in contemporary culture or they have fallen into disuse; therefore, it is necessary to understand them in their classical context. Each term is defined, and the terms are related to one another. Lecture Two then identifies a series of assumptions that undergird the practice of argumentation: the importance of an audience, the regulation of uncertainty, the difference between justification and proof, the cooperative nature of the enterprise, and the acceptance of risk. These assumptions provide the philosophical base for understanding what it means to argue as a means of reaching decisions.

Much of the contemporary revival of argumentation has emphasized its informal character and, hence, the inapplicability of formal logic as a model. Lecture Three thus is devoted to the differences between formal and informal reasoning. The main patterns of formal deduction—categorical, conditional, and disjunctive reasoning—are described and illustrated. The lecture identifies the limitations of formal reasoning as a prototype and explains how informal reasoning is fundamentally different.

Although the emphasis on informal reasoning may seem new, it actually has a long tradition, and Lecture Four surveys, in broad-brush fashion, how the study of argumentation has evolved from classical times to the present. Originally, argumentation was the heart and soul of rhetorical studies, and rhetoric was regarded as one of the seven basic liberal arts. During the intervening centuries, rhetoric was separated from its most intellectual elements, argumentation was taken over by philosophy, and formal logic (especially symbolic or mathematical logic) was regarded as the prototype for all reasoning. The lecture summarizes consequences of these trends and includes a discussion of several late-20th-century efforts to refocus argumentation studies.

The next seven lectures, Five through Eleven, examine aspects of argumentation strategies and tactics. Lecture Five begins this series by considering how controversies arise and how the most basic element of argument is the claim. It then defines the major components of an argument (a claim, evidence, an inference linking the evidence to the claim, and a warrant authorizing the inference) and describes how these components can be represented diagrammatically. Lecture Six moves from simple arguments to examine the structure of more complex arguments. Multiple, coordinative, and subordinative structures illustrate the patterns by which parts of complex arguments are brought together. We will explore how the choices among these patterns make a difference to the understanding of the overall argument.

The structures exposed in Lecture Six can be thought of as ways to map an arguer's case, that is, the set of arguments that he or she brings forward to support or oppose a claim. Lecture Seven considers the arguer's responsibility to speak to all the relevant issues in the assembly of the case. This consideration will lead into a discussion of the nature of issues, means of identifying issues in a specific case, and why addressing the issues meets the initial burden of proof. The lecture then shifts from responsibilities to choices and focuses on the arguer's options with respect to selection and arrangement of arguments.

Lectures Eight through Ten concern the processes of attacking and defending arguments, processes that collectively are known as refutation. We begin by considering the key concept of *stasis*. This concept refers to the focal point of the argument, which is created by the confrontation of assertion and denial. The first step in responding to an argument, then, is to identify the desired *stasis*. This lecture explores how different choices about *stasis* affect argument, both in the legal setting in which it was originally devised and in nonlegal arguments as well.

Lecture Nine introduces the processes of attack and defense, pointing out that, despite the military metaphor, these are cooperative activities. Choices regarding the selection of arguments for attack and the development of the attack are considered in some detail. Lecture Ten completes the discussion of attacks, then examines the process of defending and rebuilding arguments, in which the choices available to the advocate are far fewer. The lecture concludes with general techniques of refutation that can be used both by the attack and by the defense.

The treatment of argument strategy and tactics concludes with Lecture Eleven, which is devoted entirely to the role of language in argument. By considering the role of definitions, figures of speech, precision, and intensity, the lecture establishes that language is integral to argument, not ornamentation that is added to language-free content.

In the next set of seven lectures, Lectures Twelve through Eighteen, the focus shifts from argument strategy and tactics to the more microscopic level, in which specific components of the individual argument are the units of analysis, and the goals are to examine how the components are used and which factors of each component may strengthen or undermine the argument in which it is used. A single lecture examines evidence, which is discussed with reference to examples, statistical measures, objective data and historical documents, and testimony. Then six lectures address different kinds of inferences and warrants. These are especially important because they are the most complex parts of the argument and designate different argument schemes. Six different inferential patterns are examined carefully—example, analogy, sign, cause, commonplaces, and form. In each case, the lectures explain that the inference depends on probability rather than certainty. The basic pattern of the inference is described, its uses are considered, and tests are offered that help to determine whether the inference is likely to be sound. Unlike deductive reasoning, in which the soundness of an argument is a purely formal question, in argumentation the soundness of an inference is governed heavily by context and experience. After presentation of these six basic patterns of inductive inference, several hybrid inferential patterns are considered in Lecture Eighteen—reasoning with rules, reasoning about values, and dissociations.

Because the goal in constructing arguments is to have not only some sort of reasoning structure but one that will influence critical listeners, the appraisal of arguments becomes the focus of Lectures Nineteen and Twenty. These lectures offer different approaches to the question, "What makes an argument valid?" Lecture Nineteen introduces the concept of validity by reference to formal argument, then considers what errors in each of the six informal inference patterns will make an argument invalid, and finally considers general errors of vacuity that result in "empty" arguments. Lecture Twenty resumes consideration of general fallacies by considering fallacies of clarity (the use of unclear or equivocal language) and fallacies of relevance (drawing inferences from factors having nothing to do with the relationship between evidence and claim). It then circles back on the concept of fallacy by showing that supposedly fallacious inferences are sometimes valid, depending on the context, and by suggesting that validity may be more a matter of procedure than of form. In this view, valid arguments are those that enhance the purpose of resolving disagreement. Examples are offered of normative standards for arguments that follow from this position.

The final group of lectures moves to an even more macro level and considers the practice of argumentation in society. Lecture Twenty-One presents the concept of argument spheres in which different expectations shape the culture of arguing. It then addresses the nature of argumentation in the personal sphere. Lecture Twenty-Two is devoted to the technical sphere, where argumentation takes place in specialized fields. The concept of *argument field* is presented, and examples are drawn from the fields of law, science, management, ethics, and religion. Lecture Twenty-Three deals with the public sphere, in which matters of general interest are discussed, and the public participates in its capacity as citizenry. This lecture also explores the relationship between a robust public sphere and a healthy democracy.

Finally, Lecture Twenty-Four returns to the level of generality with which the series began and considers how arguments terminate and then explores the larger goals served by argumentation as a process

4

of human interaction. Most significantly, argumentation is a means of collective judgment and decision making, and hence of governance. It also is a way of knowing and a means to the achievement of the goals of democratic life. As the conclusion notes, although it is sometimes thought fashionable to demean an *argument culture* as inimical to harmony and civil peace, a culture of argumentation is actually something to be embraced in a world in which important decisions must be made under conditions of uncertainty.

Lecture One
Introducing Argumentation and Rhetoric

Scope:

In everyday usage, *argumentation* often has negative connotations, suggesting quarrelsomeness and unpleasantness. We must put this stereotype aside and examine argumentation in its classical sense—as the study of effective reasoning. This introductory lecture will explain just what this idea means. It also will relate argumentation to the field of rhetoric. *Rhetoric* is another term that has taken on pejorative connotations but that has a rich history as the study of how messages influence people. Argumentation is also related to two other fields, *logic* and *dialectic*, that will be explained in this lecture. We also will consider the question of how argumentation is ethical. With a clear understanding of these basic terms, we will be ready to launch our study, and the lecture will preview the directions we will take.

Outline

I. Argumentation is the study of effective reasoning.

   A. Popular conceptions of argumentation as unpleasant and quarrelsome need to be set aside.

   B. Arguing is reason giving.
   1. Reasons are justifications or support for claims.
   2. Rationality is the ability to engage in reason giving.
   3. The alternative to reason giving is to accept or reject claims on whim or command.

   C. To talk about *effective* reasoning is to imply concern for an audience.
   1. Arguments are not offered in a vacuum.
   2. Success ultimately depends on the assent of an audience.
   3. Assent is based on audience acceptance of the reasoning.
   4. Hence argumentation is one way in which we attempt to persuade.

   D. It is possible, though, to conduct an argument with oneself.

II. Argumentation is a common but imperiled activity.

    A. It is sometimes thought that, because everyone does it, argumentation does not require careful study.

        1. Argumentation indeed is pervasive in daily life.

        2. It occurs everywhere from informal encounters between people to the formally structured debate.

    B. A recent newspaper column suggests, however, that argumentation may be a lost art.

        1. People increasingly interact only with those who agree with them.

        2. Differences of opinion are treated as unbridgeable.

        3. The result is to weaken opportunities for compromise, deliberation, and mutual understanding.

        4. Argumentation is the antidote.

    C. The difference between productive arguments and destructive quarrels often is in the understanding of principles.

III. Argumentation is both a product and a process.

    A. Sometimes our focus is on messages, the products of argumentation.

        1. Messages are both explicit and implicit.

        2. They are capable of being cast into language.

        3. They are capable of analysis and appraisal.

    B. Sometimes our focus is on interaction, the process of argumentation.

        1. Argumentation is an interaction in which people maintain what they think are mutually exclusive positions, and they seek to resolve their disagreement.

        2. They seek to convince each other, but at the same time they are open to influence themselves.

        3. We study how they go about convincing others and how their efforts might be more productive.

IV. Argumentation is the field of study in which rhetoric, logic, and dialectic meet.

    A. From rhetoric we derive our concern with the audience.

1. Today, rhetoric often has negative connotations, including insincerity, vacuity, bombast, and ornamentation.
2. The classical understanding of rhetoric is the study of how messages influence people; it focuses on the development and communication of knowledge between speakers and listeners.
3. "Thinking rhetorically" means reasoning with audience predispositions in mind.

B. From logic we derive our concern with form and structures of reasoning.
1. Today, logic is often mistakenly seen as encompassing only formal symbolic and mathematical reasoning.
2. Informal logic, from which argumentation borrows, is grounded in ordinary language and describes reasoning patterns that lack the certainty of mathematics.

C. From dialectic we derive our concern with deliberation.
1. Today, dialectic is often understood as the grand sweep of opposing historical forces, such as the clash between capitalism and communism.
2. In fact, the term refers to a process of discovering and testing knowledge through questions and answers.
3. Although Plato's dialogues are the models of dialectic, any conversation that is a critical discussion will qualify.

V. Ethical considerations figure prominently in argumentation.

A. Any attempt to influence other people raises ethical issues.
1. It is a limitation on freedom of choice.
2. It is the application of superior to inferior force.

B. But argumentation seeks to achieve ethical influence.
1. It does not influence people against their will but seeks their free assent.
2. Without influence, the conditions of society and community are not possible.
3. Argumentation respects different ways of thinking and reasoning.

VI. This series of lectures will explore the nature of argumentation.

A. We will try to accomplish several goals.

1. We will learn a vocabulary that helps us to recognize and describe argumentation.
2. We will become aware of the significance of choice and will broaden our understanding of the choices available to arguers.
3. We will develop standards for appraising arguments and explaining what will make them better.
4. We will examine a variety of historical and contemporary arguments as examples.
5. We should improve our abilities both as analysts and as makers of arguments.

B. We will follow an organizational plan.
   1. We will begin by reviewing the assumptions underlying argumentation and the historical development of the field.
   2. We then will explore strategies and tactics of argument construction, attack, and defense.
   3. We will consider the components of argument in more detail and consider how they work.
   4. We will investigate the concept of validity and consider fallacies in argumentation.
   5. Finally, we will investigate how argumentation functions in society—in the personal, technical, and public spheres.

Essential Reading:

"Argumentation," in Thomas O. Sloane, ed., *Encyclopedia of Rhetoric*, pp. 33–37.

Chaim Perelman, *The Realm of Rhetoric*, pp. 1–20.

Supplementary Reading:

Daniel J. O'Keefe, "The Concepts of Argument and Arguing," in J. Robert Cox and Charles Arthur Willard, eds., *Advances in Argumentation Theory and Research*, pp. 3–23.

James A. Herrick, *Argumentation: Understanding and Shaping Arguments*, pp. 49–60.

Frans H. van Eemeren et al., *Fundamentals of Argumentation Theory: A Handbook of Historical Backgrounds and Contemporary Developments*, pp. 1–26, 98–102.

Questions to Consider:

1. How has the pejorative connotation of *argumentation* limited our understanding of the field of study?

2. If the audience ultimately is the judge of argument, how can we avoid equating sound argument with whatever happens to persuade a particular audience?

Lecture One—Transcript
Introducing Argumentation and Rhetoric

It's a pleasure to welcome you to a series of 24 lectures on argumentation in which we'll explore the study of effective reasoning. If we've met in a previous course, it's good to be back with you. If not, let me say hello at this time. In either case, I hope that you will enjoy this experience. Courses in this subject are offered sometimes in English departments; sometimes in Philosophy departments; sometimes, as in my case, in Communications Studies departments, where I've taught at Northwestern University for almost 40 years.

Often when I mention that I teach argumentation, people will ask, "You mean you actually teach that? Why would anybody want to study that?" That reflects the fact that in contemporary English usage the terms "argue" and "argument" have, often, unfavorable connotations. When a parent says to a child, "Don't argue with me about that," arguing is not something that's thought of as very pleasant; or when a superior and a subordinate in a business relationship engage in an argument, that's seen sometimes as destructive. We often think of arguing as unpleasant or quarrelsome. We sometimes see disagreement as unhealthy. We sometimes talk about it in military terms, as though our goal were to conquer an opponent or to vanquish an adversary. When we express disagreement, it's sometimes seen as rancorous or bitter; somehow destructive of the self-worth of another person. Please, rest assured; neither The Teaching Company nor I seek to promote such a view, which is, after all, a perversion of what argumentation really is. Let's set that aside at the outset, and explore argumentation as the study of effective reasoning.

Arguing is reason giving. What do I mean by reason giving? When people speak to one another, or with an audience in mind, they make claims. They make statements that they believe, and that they would like for their listeners or their readers to believe as well. We make claims about matters that are uncertain, that we cannot establish absolutely or definitely.

For example, we might say it's better to build a missile defense system than to rely on an antiballistic missile treaty, or vice versa. We might say energy shortages can be overcome through conservation alone, or not. We might say that in the long run children learn read to better if they're taught by phonics rather than by whole language, or the reverse. We might say that changes in gender roles over the past generation, on balance, have been beneficial or harmful. Each of these is a claim. It's a statement that we assert as our belief and that we want another person to believe as well.

Reasons are the justifications that we give for those claims. They're not absolute proofs, because each of these matters is somehow inherently uncertain. It depends upon a value judgment; or it relates to the future; or it's so large that it can't be seen directly; so we try to justify our claims by giving reasons for them. Hence, we could say that arguing is the practice of justifying claims, and that's certainly one way to look at what it is that we will be studying.

If we think about it for a minute, what's the alternative to reason giving? It's to accept or reject claims in knee-jerk fashion based on whim, or caprice, or on the command of an authority figure. If we do that, then we are dismissing to the realm of chance, or accident, or happenstance, or coercion some very important aspects of human affairs; when we make judgments, when we make predictions, when we make large global kinds of claims. We don't want to do that. We don't want to dismiss all of these areas to the realm of the accidental. Indeed, when we think about it, what makes us rational is the ability to engage in reason giving, to connect the claims that we make to the justifications for them. And so we can say, argumentation is the study of effective reasoning.

Once I stick in this term "effective," we have to ask, effective for whom? This implies a concern for an audience. We don't offer claims or reasons in a vacuum. We offer them with a reader, or a listener, or a large public in mind. Indeed, the success of the arguments ultimately depends upon the assent of the audience.

What do I mean when I talk about the assent of an audience? Again, I don't mean a knee-jerk agreement, or an instantaneous rejection, or a reaction that says in effect, "Wow that agrees with my prejudice." What I mean by "assent" is adherence to the claim based on the reasons for it. When I talk about an audience adhering or giving its assent to an argument, I'm suggesting that the audience accepts the reason. It accepts the grounds that are given; the justifications that are given; and the connection that's made between these justifications and the claim. Argumentation is, then, one of the ways that we seek to persuade others. And while I focus on persuading others, it's also possible to have an argument with oneself, to ask questions, and raise challenges to one's own view, so that we will be forced to justify it.

What I've suggested so far is that we cast aside a notion of arguing as quarrelsome or rancorous and disagreeable, and instead of think of it as the practice of giving reasons to justify claims seeking the adherence of an audience. If we think about it that way, we'll realize argumentation is something that we engage in all the time. We talk with another person; any time we write; any time we seek to influence what another person or group of people thinks, or believes, or does.

That presents us, in a way, with a second problem in understanding what argumentation is all about. If we do it all the time, if it's a natural human activity, why do we need to study it? Why do we need to teach it? It's just something we do naturally. I am assuming that you don't share this view, because if you did, you probably wouldn't have bought this course. So there's a sense in which I'm preaching to the converted. Argumentation is a skill we can understand and improve.

Skillful argumentation, indeed, is an imperiled activity. In June of 2005, an op-ed editorial in the *New York Times* suggested that argumentation may be a lost art. It said people increasingly interact only with those who already agree with them. Differences of opinion are treated as unbridgeable. The result is to weaken opportunities for compromise, deliberation, and mutual understanding. Understanding and practicing argumentation is the antidote to these destructive behaviors. The difference between arguments that are productive—arguments in which people give claims, make claims, give reasons, exchange reasons—and arguments that are not—arguments that invoke all these negative stereotypes of bickering and quarreling—often is the understanding of the principles that underlie this common human activity. These lectures will enable us to understand the underlying principles and theories.

Argumentation is both a product and the process, and we use the same term to refer to both. When we engage in argumentation, we make arguments, and we have arguments. These are two different perspectives about what's going on. They reflect the fact that argumentation involves the production and exchange of messages in interaction with other people.

Sometimes, we want to study the message—the product of argumentation. Messages sometimes take the form of formal texts—a speech, a newspaper editorial, a transcript of a Presidential debate or a Congressional hearing—but sometimes the texts are much less formal. If we have a conversation with someone else, the text of the conversation is the message even though we typically don't write it down. Sometimes the argument is not explicitly verbal. The message could be a shrug of the shoulders that conveys the claim that we want to make: "This isn't really that important;" or, "I don't really care that much about it;" or, "It doesn't make that much difference." Non-verbal cues may imply arguments. Sometimes there'll be a text that's explicit, and yet there will be all sorts of unstated assumptions that are also parts of the argument.

So, the message is both explicit and implicit. It's verbal, sometimes nonverbal; but it's capable, at least, of being cast into language, so that we can examine it as a structure of claims and justifications. One view of argument focuses on the product, the message. In several of the lectures in this series, that's what we will be doing.

But it's also possible to focus on the interaction with other people. When we focus on that, we're stressing not the product, not the outcome of the argument, but the process of arguing itself. When we look at it this way, what we see is a kind of interaction in which people maintained what they think are mutually exclusive propositions. What I mean by that, simply, is that the participants in an argument hold views that they think can't be reconciled. If they could be reconciled easily, that's what they would do; and that would be the end of the matter. They believe that they can't be reconciled, but they also want to resolve this disagreement. They may or may not succeed, but they want to. They don't regard it as a trivial matter. They don't simply say, "Well, I believe this, and you believe that, and that's fine." They want somehow to come to some common understanding. They seek to convince each other by giving reasons to justify their views; and at the same they do that, they're open to the possibility of being influenced themselves. From this perspective, we study how people go about doing this, and how their efforts might be made more productive.

Arguing has a two-faced character: argument is a product, and argument is a process. Sometimes we'll be talking about the products—the texts—and sometimes about the process—the interaction between people.

As a field of study, argumentation draws on three root disciplines, each of which itself is often misunderstood: rhetoric, logic, and dialectic. From rhetoric, we derive our concern with the audience. Unfortunately, just as argument in popular culture has negative connotations, so does rhetoric. It's sometimes associated with bombast; with emptiness; with phrases that don't mean anything; with ornate and flowery language; or worst of all, freshman composition, that dread course, Rhetoric 101. Once again, these are misconceptions of what rhetoric is about.

We need to restore a conception of rhetoric that goes all the way back to the classical period, to ancient Greece. We'll explore the origins of rhetoric much more in Lecture Four, but we can say some things about it right off the bat. Rhetoric focuses on how speakers (or writers) and listeners (or readers) develop and communicate knowledge. By knowledge, I don't mean what's timeless and eternally true; but what the listeners, what those who interact, what the participants regard as true, and accept as true are willing to believe and to act upon.

So, rhetoric studies how people together create, develop, and communicate knowledge. It's the study of how messages influence people. We can immediately see from this definition that argumentation is a subset of that, exploring how people are influenced by reason giving. Obviously, messages influence people in all sorts of other ways as well—by their style, their presentation, their emotional appeals, and so on. Argumentation focuses on reason giving.

It was Aristotle who defined rhetoric as the faculty or skill of discovering the available means of persuasion in a given case. In this sense, it is an analytical skill. It's an art of figuring out, in a situation in which we find ourselves, the resources that we could draw upon to make claims that would influence other people through the process of reason.

Until fairly recently, rhetoric was not regarded as pejorative as all; it was seen as a noble activity. Rhetoric was one of the seven original liberal arts. We're going to restore that conception of rhetoric for the purpose of this series of lectures, and when we do that we will be thinking rhetorically about arguments. When we think rhetorically, we're in a certain frame of mind that says we're paying attention to an audience. We will need to know what the audience predispositions are, because we reason from them. It means that we have to recognize the role of choices on the part of speakers and listeners. We have to recognize that the influence of listeners is non-coercive. We don't bludgeon into submission. We influence them, when we do, by making claims and giving reasons that they will find justifiable and acceptable, to which they will want to give their adherence. Thus, argumentation takes from rhetoric a concern with the audience.

There are two other fields of study to which argumentation is related. One of these is logic, another term that we sometimes misconstrue. Particularly in the last couple of centuries, logic has been associated with formal symbolic logic or mathematical reason. When people study logic in schools these days, it's often not as it is studied in a mathematics class, with p's and q's; and truth tables; and if this, then certainly that; and that is, indeed, one branch of reason. But, in fact, logic is concerned with all structures of reason, whether they are formal or not.

In the second half of the 20th century, in particular, we've seen the development of a whole sub-field of study known as informal logic; that is, reasoning that doesn't have certainty; that isn't mathematical; that's not divorced from the content of the statements being made. As we can probably see right away, informal logic is close cousin of argumentation; because what after all are we doing when we engage in argument? We're creating and using structures of reasoning, structures that connect reasons, and claims that are not formal in nature and that don't have the certainty that's associated with mathematics. So, we have rhetoric and logic.

The other field that I want to mention is dialectic. Here's another one that we sometimes misunderstand. When we think of dialectic, we often think almost in the sense that Karl Marx wrote about as the grand sweep of opposing historical forces, such as that between capitalism and communism, that will be a thesis and antithesis, in which there would be a resolution, a grand new synthesis. Yes, that's one sense of what dialectic means; but the term, again, is much broader than that. It refers most generally to the process of discovering and testing knowledge through questions and answers.

Of course, in this understanding, the very model of dialectic is the dialogues of Plato, in which the Platonic Socrates encounters an interlocutor or another; the person states a view; Plato has Socrates ask a series of questions; and through the exchange of questions and answers, the view is tested, or elaborated, or clarified.

We often think of the courtroom as another place where this kind of dialectical procedure takes place, through the act of cross examination: a series of questions and answers to try to figure out what's ultimately the truth of the case. For that matter, any conversation that's a critical discussion in which people are thinking critically and carefully will qualify as employing dialectic, as a kind of testing through question and answer.

From rhetoric, argumentation derives its concern with the audience. From logic, it derives the concern with structures of reason. And from dialectic, it derives a process of testing knowledge through question and answer in an iterative way. We might say that argumentation is the field of study where logic, dialectic, and rhetoric all meet. We've got this family of four terms: argumentation, rhetoric, logic, and dialectic, each of them often subject to misunderstanding; but if we understand them correctly, they'll point the way to a very important field of study and a very important human endeavor as well. This is the field of study upon which these lectures will focus.

There's another term that we need to examine, and that's the term ethics. Any attempt to influence other people necessarily raises some ethical questions. After all, if I try to get you to do something or to believe something, it's a limitation on your freedom of choice. I'm not leaving you alone to do whatever you want; I'm trying to induce you to do what I want. And what's more, it's the application of superior to inferior force, even if the force is intellectual and persuasive rather than physical. And so an attempt to limit other people's freedom of choice and to impose superior on inferior force automatically raises questions about whether it's ethical to do.

Again, please rest assured, neither The Teaching Company nor I knowingly promote unethical activity. In fact, argumentation seeks to achieve ethical influence. What is it that makes it ethical? For starters, it does not influence other people against their will. It seeks their free assent. It seeks their agreement to a claim on the basis that they have to come to accept the reasons for the claim and the connection between the reasons and the claim. It seeks free assent.

Moreover, what's the alternative? If there were no attempts to influence people, then the conditions of society and community would not be possible. Everyone would go his or her own separate way with no sense of social cohesion, no bonds with others. What is it that creates the bonds with others on which communities and societies are built? It's the interaction between people in which we relate to and try to influence others.

So it won't do to say that any attempt to influence other people is to be questioned, because we can't avoid influencing other people. The issue is how we go about it. It's my belief that the most ethical way to go about influencing other people is through argumentation, which respects their individuality, and respects their freedom, and seeks their free assent. Argumentation respects listeners, and it respects that they have different ways of thinking and reasoning. I hope and I trust that this study on which we are about to embark is indeed an ethical as well as a noble activity.

Before I conclude this first lecture, let me talk specifically about what you can expect to accomplish from this course and how we will go about it. I sometimes get calls or e-mails from people saying, "Could you please teach me how to win more arguments with my spouse?" and the answer is, "No. I'm not going to do that." What I hope is, that as result of the material that we'll be considering, you and your spouse, if you have one, will both be able to have more productive and more constructive arguments, and turn them into win-win situations, where you both come out ahead. This is not a course in how to overpower your spouse, or your significant other, or your friend.

Sometimes I get calls saying, "Would you please tell me how to prove to an atheist that God exists?" or "How to prove to a religious person that there is no God." Again, the answer is, "No. I'm not going to do that."

What we will see as we go through these lectures is that arguments depend, at a very basic level on common frames of reference. If we have a situation in which there is such disparity in the frame of reference that there's nothing in common as between an atheist and a religious person about whether there is a God, there's nothing really for argument to do about that. So we're not going to do those sorts of things.

What are we going to do and what can you get from it? There are five specific goals that I hope you'll achieve through this series of lectures. First, we'll learn to recognize arguments when we see them. We'll learn a vocabulary that helps us to describe argumentation, not in order to give us a whole lot of jargon, but to enable us to understand and talk about what it is that people do when the argue. The first thing we'll do is, we'll learn how to recognize arguments; how to find them in conversations, in newspaper editorials, in speeches, in controversies of any kind; and how to know them when we see them.

Second, we'll become aware of how people, when they argue, make choices. Every time people engage in argumentation, they could go about it in lots of different ways, and they make choices. They may make them knowingly and deliberately or not, but they make choices. Hopefully, we will become aware of how arguing reflects choice, and we'll broaden our understanding of the choices that arguers can make, that you can make, when you build and construct arguments.

Third, we'll learn something about how to appraise arguments, how to evaluate them. We talk about good arguments, bad arguments, strong arguments, weak arguments, better arguments, worse arguments; and so, part of what we'll do is discuss how we make those judgments; how we evaluate arguments, what kinds of standards govern our assessment. We do that not simply to sit and pass judgment on others, but to get a good understanding of what can make our own arguments better, as well as to see weaknesses in arguments that we object to.

Fourth, in attempting all of these tasks, we're going to examine as examples a variety of historical and contemporary arguments; and so one of the things we'll do is we'll learn more about some significant controversies by looking at them from the perspective of argument.

Finally, as a result of all of these things, we should sensitize ourselves to argumentation theories, and as a result, you should be able to improve your ability both as an analyst and as a maker of arguments.

Here's the plan for doing this: the first four lectures, including this one, will review the assumptions underlying argumentation and the development of the field. Then, in lectures five through eleven, we'll explore the strategies and tactics of argument construction, attack, and defense. In the next seven lectures, we'll consider the components of argument in more detail and how they work. We'll take two lectures to investigate the concept of validity and fallacies; and finally, we'll investigate how argumentation functions in society. I am certainly looking forward to this series of lectures. I hope that you are as well.

Lecture Two
Underlying Assumptions of Argumentation

Scope:

Argumentation is a means of decision-making, and there are several key assumptions that we make when we use it. This lecture will focus on five key assumptions. First, argumentation takes place with an audience in mind, and the audience is the ultimate judge of success or failure. Second, argumentation occurs only under conditions of uncertainty, about matters that could be otherwise. Third, argumentation involves justification (rather than proof) of ideas and beliefs, and the difference between justification and proof is crucial. Fourth, despite its seemingly adversarial character, argumentation is basically cooperative. Fifth, arguers accept risks, and their nature and significance will be explained.

Outline

I. Argumentation takes place with an audience in mind, and the audience is the ultimate judge of success or failure.

    A. Historical examples establish the significance of the audience.

        1. *The Federalist Papers* were written to influence a particular audience.

        2. The Lincoln-Douglas debates were conducted for a particular audience.

    B. These examples suggest that the claims being advanced are not universal truths but are subject to the acceptance of actual listeners.

    C. The particulars of an audience's situation will affect its values, priorities, and methods of judgment.

    D. The audience for argumentation consists of the people the arguer wants to influence—not necessarily those who are immediately present.

    E. Recognizing differences in audience beliefs does not entail accepting the idea that any belief is as good as any other.

II. Argumentation takes place under conditions of uncertainty.

    A. We do not argue about things that are certain—although even the notion of certainty is audience-dependent.

    B. Things that are uncertain are potentially controversial.

        1. *The Federalist Papers* offer a historical example.

        2. The Lincoln-Douglas debates offer a historical example.

        3. Controversies involve genuine differences of opinion that matter to the participants and which they wish to see resolved.

    C. Controversies have multiple dimensions.

        1. They may be explicit (recognized by the participants) or implicit (recognized by an analyst).

        2. They may be unmixed (only one arguer maintains a position) or mixed (multiple arguers do so).

        3. They may be single (relating only to one claim) or multiple (relating to more than one claim).

    D. Uncertainty implies that things could be otherwise; the outcome is not known for sure.

        1. Therefore, there is an inferential leap in the argument, from the known to the unknown.

        2. The audience is asked to accept this leap.

III. Argumentation involves justification for claims.

    A. Arguers offer a rationale for accepting an uncertain claim.

        1. The rationale represents reasons for making the inferential leap.

        2. The reasons are acceptable, if they can convince a reasonable person who is exercising critical judgment.

        3. If so, we say that the claim is justified.

    B. The competing narratives in the Lincoln-Douglas debates provide a historical example.

    C. To say that claims are justified entails certain implications.

        1. Justification is different from proof; it is subjective and dependent upon a particular audience.

        2. It implies that people are willing to be convinced, yet skeptical enough not to take statements on faith.

        3. Justification is always provisional and subject to change in light of new information or arguments.

4. It varies in degree of strength, ranging from merely plausible to highly probable.

IV. Despite its seemingly adversarial character, argumentation is fundamentally a cooperative enterprise.

    A. Arguers share a common goal of reaching the best possible decision under the circumstances.

    B. The adversarial elements of argument are means toward the achievement of this common goal.

        1. They improve the rigor of the procedure.

        2. They reduce the likelihood that critical details will be omitted.

        3. They increase confidence in the result.

    C. There are other matters on which arguers also agree.

        1. They share a frame of reference, some level of agreement on which their disagreement is built.

        2. They share a common language and system of meanings.

        3. They share procedural assumptions and norms, such as what counts as evidence.

        4. They share the values of modesty, respect for the audience, and the importance of free assent.

    D. *The Federalist Papers* offer a historical example.

V. Argumentation entails risks.

    A. Arguers face two principal risks.

        1. They face the risk of being shown to be wrong and hence losing the argument.

        2. They face the risk of loss of face from the perception that they have performed badly in the argument.

    B. If a person knew, for sure, that he or she was right, that person might not have an incentive to engage in argument.

        1. For example, some scholars will not engage in argument with those who seek to deny historical facts.

        2. Others will not engage in argument with those who cast doubt on generally accepted scientific theories.

    C. Conversely, the decision to engage in argumentation suggests a willingness to run the risks.

        1. Douglas's willingness to debate Lincoln offers a historical example.

2. People run the risks because they do not know, for sure, that they are right.
3. People run the risks because they value the judgment of their adversaries and want assent only if it is freely given.
   D. In valuing the personhood of the adversary, the arguer claims the same value for himself or herself.

Essential Reading:

James A. Herrick, *Argumentation: Understanding and Shaping Arguments*, pp. 63–74.

Frans H. van Eemeren et al, *Argumentation: Analysis, Evaluation, Presentation*, pp. 3–36.

Supplementary Reading:

Wayne Brockriede, "Where Is Argument?" in Robert Trapp and Janice Schuetz, eds., *Perspectives on Argumentation: Essays in Honor of Wayne Brockriede*, pp. 4–8.

Michael A. Gilbert, *Coalescent Argumentation*.

Questions to Consider:

1. If argumentation involves uncertainty, how can arguers arrive at conclusions with any degree of confidence?

2. How can people with strong but opposing convictions engage in argumentation and preserve its cooperative character?

Lecture Two—Transcript
Underlying Assumptions of Argumentation

Hello again. In the first lecture, we introduced ourselves to argumentation, opening up a field of study that is often closed off by fundamental misunderstandings. We related argumentation to a family of other terms: rhetoric, logic, and dialectic. In this lecture, I want to focus on series of assumptions that we make when we use argumentation as a means of decision making. There are five key assumptions, and I want to spend a little bit of time talking with you about each. The first is that argumentation takes place with an audience in mind, and the audience is the ultimate judge of the success or failure of arguments.

The first assumption, then, is argumentation is audience dependent. This means, of course, that it is different from statements like "two plus two equals four." which really don't depend on audience for their truth or for their acceptability. Before I explain how argumentation is audience dependent, let's look briefly at a couple of historical examples that help to make it clear, and I'm going to use these same two examples throughout the lecture.

First, *The Federalist Papers*; we think of *The Federalist Papers* often as exhibiting a philosophical perspective on American government and politics. But in fact, *The Federalist Papers* were written for the very specific purpose of influencing delegates in New York State in the ratifying convention to vote to ratify the proposed constitution, which meant that *The Federalist Papers* had to be written with an eye to what was on the mind of the prospective voters in New York, and what would be likely to sway those voters in favor of the new government. They were constructed with an audience in mind.

A second example is the Lincoln-Douglas debates. We often think of those debates as eloquent articulations of the competing views of Lincoln and Douglas about slavery; but, in fact, they were tailored to a very specific audience, to the swing voters in central Illinois who were both opposed to slavery and opposed to immediate abolition. In those debates, Lincoln and Douglas were each was trying to portray the other as an extremist—Douglas was portraying Lincoln as really an abolitionist, Lincoln portraying Douglas as really wanting to spread slavery everywhere—in order to appeal to the predispositions of the particular audience for whom they were both especially concerned.

These examples tell us that the claims that are being advanced in arguments are not universal timeless truths; they are claims that are subject to the acceptance of actual listeners. An arguer who wants to succeed with an audience must take that audience into account. The particulars of the audience's situation will affect its values, its priorities, and its methods of judgment.

Who is the audience? In one sense it's the people who are physically present to hear an argument or the people who actually read an argument, but it's often broader than that. An audience is all of the people whom the arguer seeks to affect. If we're talking about informal arguments between friends or spouses, for example, the arguments are fairly private; the audience is the people who are participating in the interaction itself. But if we imagine arguments in a more public setting, let's say on the floor of the United States Senate, a U.S. Senator is making arguments, not primarily for the benefit of the two, or three, or four, or five other senators on the floor who are physically present; he or she is using that occasion in order to make arguments that will be read by another audience, that is, the people back home whom he or she is trying to influence.

Saying that arguments are dependent on an audience is sometimes misunderstood as saying, "whatever an audience believes is fine. One argument is as good as another if you can find somebody who will accept it." This is not right; we're not talking about just telling an audience what they want to hear. In fact, as we'll go along in the series of lectures, there are all sorts of other standards that we try to meet; but it is the case that the argument must take the audience into account if it's going to have a chance to prevail. The first assumption, then, is that arguments depend upon audiences.

The second key assumption: argumentation takes places under conditions of uncertainty. We don't argue about things that are certain. Let me digress for just a second, to point out that even the notion of certainty is audience dependent. If you ask, "Is it a certainty that it's too early in the morning to have class at 8:00," you ask undergraduate students and they'll say, "Oh yes indeed." But you ask people who are accustomed to going to work at 7:00, or 7:30, or 8:00, they won't understand it. So, even certainty is somehow dependent on an audience. Some people believe that the statement "two plus two equals four" is objectively true, and some people believe it's true only because it commands universal agreement. This is very significant philosophical problem, but fortunately it's not one that we need to resolve. Whatever the source of certainty, whether it's objective truth or unanimous agreement, we don't argue about things that are certain. There are much easier ways to settle disagreements or to resolve them.

Things that are uncertain are potentially controversial; they could be otherwise, and we don't know for sure. Take for example the question, "When does life begin?" People may have fervent beliefs about that subject; they may feel intensely about it, but we don't know. It's not given to us know with certainty when life begins. If we could know it for sure, then the whole dispute about abortion would take a very different course from the one it's taken. We argue about things that we don't know for sure.

Let's again consider our historical examples. One of the subjects taken up in *The Federalist Papers* is the question, "Is a small republic or a large republic more likely to control factions?" Everybody wants to control factions. The question is, what's the best way to do it? We don't know for sure, and so the anti-federalists had argued if you look at history, its small republics that controlled factions. The authors of *The Federalist Papers* argue the opposite; actually a large republic will better control faction.

Or take the Lincoln-Douglas debates: one of the questions talked about in those debates is, "Was the Kansas Nebraska Act part of a plot to spread slavery all over the country?" By the very nature of that question you'll see that we can't know for sure. It's a speculative question. Lincoln argues that if you put this and this piece of evidence together, you'll have reasons to think that it is; and Douglas argues that it's a preposterous notion, that it's a part of a plot. These are controversial. They're uncertain. Controversies involve genuine differences of opinion that matter to the participants, and which they want to see resolved.

There are lots of ways we could look at controversies. Controversies may be explicit, that is, they're recognized as such by the people in them; or they may be implicit. It may be that only a third party, an analyst of the argument can see the controversy. For example, in the Lincoln-Douglas debate, there's an explicit controversy about whether or not the candidates support the Dred Scott Decision. But it's not made explicit that there's also disagreement between them about what the Dred Scott Decision says. That's an implicit controversy that a third party could look at their debate and see.

Controversies may be what are called unmixed, meaning that only one of the arguers maintains a position, and the other one just challenges it; or they may be mixed, meaning that each arguer maintains a position. For example, in 2005 when President Bush proposed to create individual retirement accounts as part of Social Security, the Democrats in the Senate said, "We are not going to discuss Social Security reform until you take that off the table." Only one of the arguers developed and maintained a position.

On the other hand, also in 2005, following the resignation of Supreme Justice Sandra Day O'Connor, some people argued the president ought to nominate a true conservative to that seat, and others argued the president ought to nominate a moderate to that seat. And both sets of arguers maintained and defended a position. We could have unmixed or mixed controversies. Controversies may be single, that is, they relate only to one claim at a time; or they may be multiple, relating to more than claim.

For example, when the parent says to the teenager, "You shouldn't stay out past midnight," and the teenager says to the parent, "You don't trust me." There are two different claims now, both at issue: one about what the teenager ought to do, and one about whether or not the parent trusts the child. In any event, however when we look at controversies, the uncertainty implies that the outcome is not known for sure. There's an inferential leap in the argument from the known to the unknown, and the audience, based on their judgment, is asked to accept this leap. We can't wait for things to become certain because they never will, and yet we have to reach some decision.

The first assumption of argumentation is that it's audience dependent. The second is that it's grounded in uncertainty. The third is that it involves justification for claims. Arguers offer a rational for accepting an uncertain claim. What this rational is, is the reasons for making the inferential leap from what we know to what we're not sure about. Those reasons are considered to be acceptable, if they would convince a reasonable person who is exercising critical judgment; if that happens, we say that the claim is justified. We get that judgment by giving reasons that a critical listener would accept.

The participants in an argument assume this role of critical listener for the other. If I'm arguing with you, what I want to do is, I want to give reasons that you, as critical listener, would regard as acceptable, justifiable reasons; and the thing that will best strengthen my argument is your critical abilities being brought to bear on what I have to say. Likewise, I will serve as the critical listener for you.

The adherence of the critical listener is the substitute for the certainty that we cannot possibly achieve, and it's the criticalness of the critical listener that gives us confidence in reaching our judgments, even though they are matters only of probability and not certainty. The arguers, in fact, who are engaged in this testing of ideas through critical judgment and questioning can be seen as performing an analogous role to the scientist in the laboratory who's rigorously testing claims about the empirical world. The arguers are doing it about things that we can't see or know directly or certainly.

The competing narratives in the Lincoln-Douglas Debates provide a good example of how this takes place. One of the questions in those debates is, "What did the founding fathers believe about the question of slavery in the territories?" This was an important question because everybody venerated the founding fathers; but there was no way to know because the founding fathers had not been confronted with precisely this question.

What did the advocates do? Douglas tried to justify his position by saying, look, many of the founding fathers were slave owners. They certainly would not have believed that slavery was immoral and continued to hold slaves. Therefore, he says, that's a justification for my belief that the founding fathers would have left this question up to each state and territory to decide for itself.

Lincoln, on the other hand, said, look at what the founding fathers wrote. They wrote the constitution, and you notice they never mention the word "slavery" in the constitution. Why not? Well, it must be because they disapproved of it and expected it to die out.

What each man is doing in this contest is trying to offer a justification for the position that he is taking in the contest. Justification is not the same thing as proof in the strict sense; it's subjective. It's dependent upon a particular audience. It doesn't say that something is true. It says, "You should believe it. You should accept it, and be prepared to act on that acceptance." It implies that people are willing to be convinced, and yet are skeptical enough not just to take statements on faith. It's always provisional and subject to change in the light of new information or new arguments. It has degrees of strength. There can be plausible justifications all the way up to highly probable justifications. The third assumption then is that arguers try to justify beliefs for themselves and for others.

The fourth of the underlying assumptions that we need to understand is that, despite its seemingly adversarial character, argumentation is fundamentally a cooperative enterprise. That sounds odd. We think of argument as adversarial, but let's think again. Arguers share a common goal of reaching the best possible decision under the circumstances; otherwise they wouldn't engage in argument, one would walk away; or one would impose his or her will by force. How do we account for the adversarial elements of argument? They're means toward the achievement of this common goal. They improve the rigor of the procedure. They reduce the likelihood that critical details will be omitted, or that the arguers will jump to conclusions, and they increase confidence in the result.

To achieve this common goal, as we've seen, arguers also cooperate in being critical listeners for one another. Beyond a common goal and common roles, there are still more respects in which the activity of argumentation is cooperative. All of the parties in the dispute share some level of agreement. That may seem odd when we're talking about disagreement and controversy, but disagreements are always founded on some level of agreement.

For example, take the case of Social Security reform. Participants in this controversy share the goal of keeping social security solvent, even as they disagree about what will make it so. If there weren't this bedrock agreement, they couldn't have a meaningful argument.

Another thing arguers share—it sounds trivial but it's really not— is a common language. And by that I don't mean just that they speak English, or French, or German—I'm not talking about that. I mean they share an understanding of what we mean, for example, by "solvent" in the Social Security example. If we think about unproductive arguments for a minute, in arguments where the two parties are talking past each other, never really engage each other's positions, it's often because they're not really sharing the same language. They don't mean the same things, even if they use the same terms.

For example, liberals and conservatives both say that they want courts to interpret the law justly, but they may mean very different things. Without a common language and set of meanings, the argumentation will not succeed. *The Federalist Papers* again offers a historical example of the importance of these kinds of agreement. There was a shared belief by both federalists and anti-federalists that power corrupts. There was a shared commitment to holding the Union together, a shared understanding of what virtue meant, and a shared commitment to checks and balances. The disagreements between federalists and anti-federalists took place within the context of these bedrock agreements.

What's more, arguers also share a posture, which I think can best be described as "restrained partisanship." On the one hand they're partisan: they really believe what they say; but they're restrained in the partisanship because they don't want to overpower the other person. They share a modesty that stems from the recognition that they could be wrong. They share respect for the audience or for the other person, because they value that person. They recognize the importance of free assent that's voluntarily given, that's not the result of bludgeoning or coercion of any kind. And as audiences, they share a willingness to listen and a willingness to risk being convinced. A person who comes to argument saying, "You can say whatever you want, but my mind is made up isn't really participating in an argument." That's a shadow of argument; it's going through the motions. People who engage in argumentation risk that they may be convinced, just as they seek to convince other people.

That leads directly to the fifth underlying assumption that I want to discuss. Argumentation entails risks. One is the risk of being shown to be wrong. I start off believing something; I make a claim to you; and, in the process of our interaction, you show that I'm wrong. Now, of course, our ideal is a person who's shown to be wrong, immediately acknowledges that he or she is wrong, picks up and goes right on from there. We know that being shown to be wrong can be unsettling. It can lead to loss of face. It can diminish one's own self-worth. It can diminish one's esteem in the conversation, or in the community, or in the society. So when one engages in an argument, one is taking on that risk of being shown to be wrong. One is also taking on the risk of having to alter one's system of beliefs; to take into account something new; to add something to the storehouse of beliefs that we have; to eliminate some belief;, to modify or change some belief. All those things can be psychologically disturbing. It's cognitively disturbing, particularly if it suggests that we have beliefs that are not fully consistent with one another or that aren't carefully enough worked out.

When people engage in arguing, they mutually assume those risks. If a person knew for sure that he or she was right, that person might not have an incentive to engage in argument; and indeed there are some people who on some topics will not engage in argument.

For example, some scholars will not engage in argument with those who seek to deny historical facts, such as the existence of the Holocaust, for example. Others will not engage in argument with those who cast doubt on generally accepted scientific theories. Much of the dispute between evolution and intelligent design is actually about avoiding a dispute by trying to deny the legitimacy of one or the other position. So, there is a direct relationship between risk and uncertainty. When we don't know for sure, when matters are uncertain, and yet we're willing to talk about them, to discuss them, to engage in them, it indicates that we're willing to run some risks. The decision to engage in argument suggests a willingness to run the risks.

Let's go back to the Lincoln-Douglas Debates, for example. Stephen Douglas was the front-runner. He was, by far, the better known of the two individuals. He was the incumbent U.S. Senator seeking a third term, one of the most powerful Democrats in the country. He had no political reason to agree to the challenge that Abraham Lincoln offered to debate him, except for the fact that there was this norm out on the frontier that if somebody challenged you to a debate, and you declined, it suggested that you had something to hide. That's probably the only reason we could think of for Douglas' accepting the challenge; but he did and, in accepting the challenge, he recognized that the outcome of the debates could help his position or could injure his position. It could support his commitment to popular sovereignty, or it could bring that commitment into serious challenge and cause it to be questioned. In his agreement to debate against Abraham Lincoln, he voluntarily assumed those risks.

Likewise, Lincoln, who had been traveling around the state following Douglas—Douglas would give a speech, and then Lincoln would give a speech that same night and try to capture the crowd.

Lincoln was taking on a risk. As long as he was following around and giving answers to Douglas when Douglas wasn't there to respond directly, he might not get as large an audience or as much attention, but his positions wouldn't be challenged directly. By offering the challenge to debate Douglas and by seeking that opportunity, Lincoln also took the risk that his positions would be challenged in such a way that he would be forced to acknowledge that there were errors or things that needed to be revised.

Why do people run those risks? They run them because they don't know for sure that they are right. Even if somehow they did no for sure that they were right, they run the risk because they don't want to overpower the adversary, or to bludgeon the adversary, or to coerce the adversary. That kind of victory is meaningless to them; what they want is, they want to convince the adversary by the arguments that they advance, the claims that they make, and the structure of reasons that they offer on behalf of those claims. People run these risks usually because they don't know for sure that they're right; and even if they did, because they value the judgment of their adversaries and they want assent only if assent is freely given.

There's an interesting aspect of this. If we value our adversary and we want our adversary's assent only if freely given, we could say that what we're doing by making those statements is bestowing a kind of respect of personhood on the person with whom we're engaged in argument. We may intensely disagree, and yet we value that person as a person, so that we want a voluntary assent, the kind of judgment that comes freely and without coercion. In valuing the person-hood of our opponent, our adversary—the arguer, of course—claims the same value for him or herself.

We can too easily be misled by the fact that argumentation does have adversarial elements, so that we think of it as a zero sum game in which I must lose in order for you to win; or in which how I somehow suffer as a result of what you have achieved. It's important for us to realize that when we look at a controversy and the participants in it, that while there are adversarial elements in their behavior, they're basically showing their respect for each other by taking on these risks—the risk of being wrong and the risk of needing to alter their beliefs.

We have our five key assumptions: argumentation is audience dependent; it deals with uncertainty; it involves justification for claims, not proof; it is fundamentally cooperative; and it entails risks. This view of argumentation makes it very different from reasoning in formal logic or mathematics. We'll explore those differences more fully in the next lecture.

Lecture Three
Formal and Informal Argumentation

Scope:

For much of the 20th century, the systematic study of argumentation was associated with formal logic, which achieves deductive certainty at the price of limited relevance to everyday affairs. This lecture will review the defining features of deduction and induction and will summarize three major forms of deductive reasoning: categorical, conditional, and disjunctive. Recent years have seen renewed interest in the study of informal reasoning, which depends on probabilities. Informal reasoning is inherently uncertain, but it characterizes reasoning in most areas of human activity. The lecture will conclude by emphasizing why informal reasoning undergirds much contemporary study of argumentation.

Outline

I. Formal argument is deductive in nature.

    A. The conclusion follows necessarily from the premises.

    B. The conclusion contains no information not already present (at least implicitly) in the premises.

    C. These properties suggest two corollaries.

        1. Deductive reasoning is analytic; it requires no reference to the external world, and it may be counterfactual.

        2. Deductive reasoning does not add to our store of knowledge; it merely rearranges it.

II. The basic unit of reasoning in formal argument is the syllogism, a structure consisting of two premises and a conclusion.

    A. Categorical syllogisms contain statements that relate categories to other categories.

        1. The statements may be universal or partial.

        2. The statements may be inclusive or exclusive.

        3. The only terms that identify quantity are *all, some,* and *none.*

        4. The soundness of a categorical syllogism can be tested either by drawing Venn diagrams or by applying the rules of distribution.

B. Conditional syllogisms begin with an "if-then" statement.

    1. The "if" clause is called the *antecedent,* and the "then" clause is called the *consequent.*

    2. The argument is sound if the antecedent is affirmed or the consequent is denied.

    3. Conversely, denying the antecedent or affirming the consequent will not lead to a sound argument.

C. Disjunctive syllogisms begin with an "either-or" statement.

    1. The argument accepts or rejects one of the alternatives and draws a conclusion about the other.

    2. Rejecting one option always implies accepting the other.

    3. Accepting one option implies rejecting the other when *or* is used in an exclusive sense (one or the other but not both); it implies the opposite when *or* is used in a nonexclusive sense (one or the other or both); this distinction often must be determined from the context.

III. Although regarded as the model of argumentation well into the 20th century, in recent scholarship formal reasoning is not seen as the prototype of argumentation.

A. Very seldom does one actually reason in syllogistic form.

    1. The forms of statements cannot be separated from their content.

    2. We need finer gradations of quantity than *all, some,* and *none.*

B. Most argumentation is not represented by a form in which the conclusion contains no new information.

    1. Reasoning with an audience enables its members to move from what already is known and believed to some new position.

    2. This movement involves a leap of faith that the arguer seeks to justify.

IV. Informal reasoning, therefore, functions as the model for everyday argumentation.

A. The argument cannot be extracted from the language in which it is cast.

B. The conclusion contains new information not present in the premises.

C. The conclusion does not follow with certainty but relies on some degree of probability.

D. The conclusion can be asserted with confidence if the arguer adheres to the conventions of informal reasoning, which are based on accumulated experience.

E. Though eclipsed in the recent past, informal reasoning has a long history, as we will see in the next lecture.

Essential Reading:

"Logic," "Syllogism," in Thomas O. Sloane, ed., *Encyclopedia of Rhetoric*, pp. 450–456, 761–763.

Robert J. Fogelin and Walter Sinnott-Armstrong, *Understanding Arguments: An Introduction to Informal Logic*, pp. 115–199.

Supplementary Reading:

James A. Herrick, *Argumentation: Understanding and Shaping Arguments*, pp. 75–95.

Ralph H. Johnson, *Manifest Rationality: A Pragmatic Theory of Argument*, chapter 3.

Ray E. McKerrow, "Rationality and Reasonableness in a Theory of Argumentation," in J. Robert Cox and Charles Arthur Willard, eds., *Advances in Argumentation Theory and Research*, pp. 105–122.

Questions to Consider:

1. Under what circumstances can an argument that proceeds from general to specific be inductive? Under what circumstances can an argument that proceeds from specific to general be deductive?

2. Is informal reasoning a weaker mode than formal reasoning? Why or why not?

Diagram 3-1

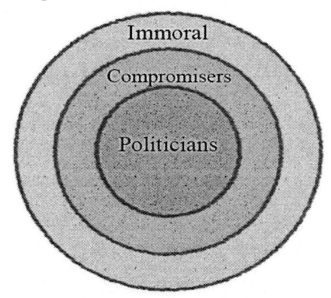

Diagram 3-2

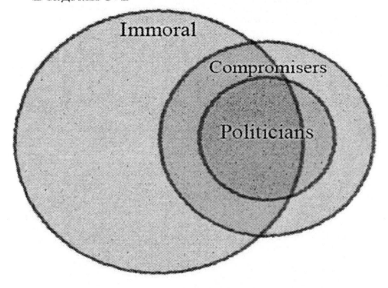

Lecture Three—Transcript
Formal and Informal Argumentation

In the last lecture, we surveyed the basic assumptions underlying argumentation theory and practice. I have mentioned several times already that argumentation deals with the uncertain. That does not sound at all like the certainty we associate with formal logic. As you may have guessed, one of my central themes is that we cannot regard formal reasoning as the model for all the kinds of reasoning in which we engage in argumentation. The time has come now to explore that claim more carefully, to see what formal reasoning is and why it is not a suitable model for everyday argument. We need to know enough about it in order to know both of these things. So, in this lecture, what I hope to do, without becoming too technical or too long, is to explore the properties of formal reasoning, the typical patterns, and then to see what the limitations of formal reasoning are as a model for argumentation.

The basic property of formal reasoning is that it is deductive in nature. Now, often, back in school, we learned that deductive and inductive reasoning were different according to the following: deductive reasoning proceeds from general to specific, and inductive reasoning proceeds from specific to general. The only problem with that is that it is wrong! Either one could do either.

Deductive reasoning is reasoning that has two basic characteristics. First, the conclusion follows necessarily, automatically, from the premises. If the premises are true, the conclusion has to be true. Now, notice that I am not saying that the premises are true. We don't care whether they are true or not. But if they are, then the conclusion must be true. To have true premises and a false conclusion in deductive reasoning would be an impossibility. The second feature of deductive reasoning is that the conclusion contains no new information; there is nothing in the conclusion that is not present, at least implicitly, in the premises. The conclusion tells us nothing new that we did not already know from the premises. So, those are the two features of deduction. If the premises are true, the conclusion must be true; and the conclusion gives us no new information.

From these two features we can derive two other corollaries—that is, two other ways to describe deductive reasoning. First of all, we can say deductive reasoning is analytic in nature, by which I mean, it does not require any reference to the external world or to any actually existing things. We can use symbols, and we often do, when we engage in deductive reasoning. "All A is B. All B is C. Therefore, all A is C." It does not make any difference what A, B, and C are, and it does not make any difference whether any of those statements is true.

Deductive reasoning, then, requires no reference to the external world, and it can even be counterfactual. My favorite example that I often use to illustrate is this: consider the following: "All heavenly bodies are made of green cheese. The moon is a heavenly body. Therefore, the moon is made of green cheese." It is absolutely good deductive reasoning, even though it is counterfactual. As far as we know, the moon is not made of green cheese or anything like it, but the form of the argument is perfect. So, deduction is analytic. It doesn't require any reference to the external world and it can even be counterfactual.

The other corollary is that deductive reasoning does not add to our store of knowledge; it merely rearranges what we already know. If we already knew that all heavenly bodies were made of green cheese and that the moon is a heavenly body, then even though we did not know it explicitly, we would know that the moon is made of green cheese. All deductive reasoning does is rearrange what we know by making explicit what may have been implicit knowledge by bringing to the foreground what may have been background knowledge. That is a quick overview, then, of deduction. Formal reasoning is deductive. The conclusion follows necessarily from the premises and it contains no new information.

What are the basic patterns of deductive or formal reasoning? The basic unit is the syllogism. You have probably heard the term syllogism. All it means is a structure consisting of at least two premises and then a conclusion that is drawn from them. If we were exploring formal reasoning more extensively, if that were the focus of our whole course, we would quickly see that there are different kinds of syllogisms. I want to highlight the basic differences.

The first kind is the categorical syllogism, and it is composed of categorical statements. These are statements that relate categories of things to other categories of things; hence, the name categorical. The categorical statements could be either universal or partial. Let's consider a simple example: the categories of politicians and compromisers. We could say, "All politicians are compromisers." It is a universal statement that takes all of one category and puts it into another category. Or, we could say, "No politicians are compromisers." It takes all of one category and keeps it out of the other category. These are universal statements. We could also say, "Some politicians are compromisers," or "Some politicians are not compromisers." These are only partial statements. So, categorical statements could be universal, applying to a whole category; or partial, applying to only a part of one.

Likewise, if you think about these same four examples, some of them are inclusive: they take all or some of one category and put it into the other category. Some of the statements are exclusive: they take all or some of one category and keep it out of the other category. Notice something else about those four statements: the only terms that we could use to measure or to quantify are "all," "none," and "some." There is no allowing for degrees between "all" and "none;" it is all encompassed by the term "some." That is as far as we can go with measuring categorical statements.

What does a categorical syllogism do? It takes these categorical statements and puts them together in premise and conclusion structures. Consider a simple example: "All politicians are compromisers. All compromisers are immoral. Therefore, all politicians are immoral." Now, remember once again, we are not concerned whether the statements are true. I hope they are not. But if all politicians are compromisers and if all compromisers are immoral, then it must be the case that all politicians are immoral. We can easily see why that is a sound, valid argument if you imagine how we might diagram it. We might draw one circle that represents politicians. We put that inside another circle representing compromisers, because all of the politicians fall within the category of compromisers. Then, we put the term compromisers into a larger circle representing immoral, because we said all compromisers are immoral. You would immediately see, once we put the compromisers' circle into the immoral circle, we have put all the politicians there, because they were all inside the compromisers' circle in the first place. You can draw diagrams like that to see whether the argument is sound or not. Or, there are elaborate rules that can be applied to determine its soundness. If we were studying formal logic for the whole course, we would go into those.

What becomes a little harder to work out, though, is a categorical syllogism like this one: "All politicians are compromisers. Some compromisers are immoral." Now, what about the conclusion? Can we conclude that some politicians are immoral? Must that conclusion be true if the premises are true? No, and we can see why. Imagine our circles again. We draw a circle for politicians, and we put all the politicians inside the circle for compromisers just like we did before. But now we have said only some compromisers are immoral, which means there would be some overlap between the circle for compromisers and the circle for that which is immoral. Now, when we are drawing the circle for immoral, we don't know whether it overlaps the part of the compromisers' circle that includes the politicians, or whether it doesn't. So, we cannot say with certainty either that some politicians are immoral or that no politicians are immoral, or that all politicians are immoral or that some politicians are not immoral. We don't know. We cannot conclude with certainty. Somebody who tried to would not be making a valid argument. That is the categorical syllogism. It takes statements that relate categories and puts them together into premise and conclusion structures.

A second kind of syllogism is called conditional or sometimes hypothetical. This is a syllogism that, instead of relating categories, starts off with an "if, then" statement. Consider this suitably nonpartisan example: "If a 'republocrat' is elected, prices will rise." We have an "if, then" statement with two parts—an "if" clause, which is called the antecedent, and a "then" clause, which is called the consequent. Then, the syllogism proceeds either to affirm or deny either the "if" or the "then" clause.

For example, looking at the "if" clause we might say, "If a republocrat is elected, prices will rise. A republocrat is elected; therefore, prices will rise." We have affirmed the antecedent. Again, the conclusion would be absolutely necessarily true given that the premises are true. If that is the case, that if the republocrat is elected, prices will rise, then if a republocrat is elected, then prices will rise. However, suppose we deny the antecedent. "If a republocrat is elected, prices will rise." A republocrat is not elected. Can we say anything about prices? No, they might rise anyway. We haven't said what would happen under those circumstances. They might or might not rise. So, if we affirm the antecedent, we have a sound or valid argument; but if we deny the antecedent, we don't.

What about the consequent, which is the "then" part of the "if, then" statement? "If a republocrat is elected, prices will rise." Prices will rise. Therefore, can we then conclude a republocrat is elected? No, because, again, prices could rise anyway whether or not a republocrat is elected. So, while affirming the antecedent, the "if" part is a valid form of argument; affirming the consequent is not a valid form of argument. Indeed, it is a very common fallacious form of argument to affirm the consequent. But, what if we deny the consequent? "If a republocrat is elected, prices will rise." Prices won't rise. Therefore, can we conclude that a republocrat is not elected? Yes, we can, because we said that if one were elected, prices would rise. Prices did not rise, so it must be the case that there was not a republocrat elected. So, with this kind of syllogism, affirming the antecedent—the "if" clause—and denying the consequent—the "then" clause—become acceptable forms of reason. But affirming the consequent or denying the antecedent are not. One more time: affirming the antecedent—saying that the "if" clause is true—and denying the consequent—saying that the "then" clause is not true— produce valid arguments and valid forms of reason. But affirming the consequent—saying the "then" clause is true—or denying the antecedent—saying that the "if" clause is not true—does not produce valid arguments. We see why in the example, where the effect could happen anyway.

All right, so we have categorical syllogisms and conditional syllogisms. The third category of syllogisms is called disjunctive, sometimes alternative. These are syllogisms that begin with an "either, or" statement—"either this, or that." Imagine a husband and a wife trying to decide how to spend a leisurely evening: "Either we will play cards tonight or we will go to the movies." Then, the syllogism proceeds to accept or reject the one alternative, and then to draw some conclusion about the other. "Either we will play cards tonight, or we will go to the movies. We will not play cards; therefore, we will go to the movies." Is that a sound argument? Sure it is, because we said we would do one or the other. We have eliminated one of the options, so there is only one left. We could say the same thing in reverse: "We won't go to the movies; therefore, we will play cards." Rejecting either alternative automatically leads to accepting the other.

Now, here is the tricky part. What if we accept one of the alternatives? "Either we will play cards tonight or we will go to the movies. We will play cards; therefore, we will not go to the movies." Can we be sure of that? Maybe. Here is where we get into a tricky area. The phrase "either, or" has two different meanings. One of them is exclusive: "either A or B, but not both." One is non-exclusive: "either A or B or both" is non-exclusive. "Could we both play cards and go to the movies?" You might say, "Well, if the night is long enough, the movie is short enough, and the card game doesn't go on forever, maybe we could." In that case, it would not be valid to accept the option and conclude we have to reject one or the other.

But, sometimes, we are talking about alternatives where we cannot do both: "Either I will drive to work Monday morning or I will walk." Now, I suppose we could contort the meaning of that sentence and imagine, "Well we could drive, and then we could come back home, and then we could walk again," but, as we use the terms, we say, "All right, I am going to work Monday morning. I will either drive or walk. If I drive I know that I will not walk. Likewise, if I walk, I will not drive." If "either, or" is used in this exclusive sense, then we can accept one option and confidently reject the other. If it is used in the non-exclusive sense, we cannot automatically reject one just because we accept the other. If it is used in the non-exclusive sense, we don't know. But, we always know that if we reject one, we accept the other.

These, then, are the three patterns of syllogisms, the three common patterns of formal reasoning. One relates categories to other categories, one deals with "if, then" statements, and one deals with "either, or."

In the past 20 minutes, we have encapsulated a whole course in formal logic. I think we understand enough about formal logic to know that it is deductive in nature and to realize what that means. If the premises are true, then the conclusion must be, and the conclusion gives us no new information. Until fairly recently, as I said in the first lecture, this was regarded as the prototype for all forms of reasoning. It was seen as the model case. Other reasoning ought to aspire to the standards of formal reasoning.

This view has come under increasingly strong challenges, and the challenges take several forms. One of them is to suggest that very seldom does one actually reason in syllogistic form. Let's consider a couple of things about it. Remember, I said it requires no reference to reality. It could be done entirely in symbols: "All A is B; all B is C." How often is it the case that when we talk about things, we make claims that we can extract from reality, and it makes no difference what we are talking about? It is very seldom. In fact, most of the time, precisely what we want to talk about is the category of some specific subject matter.

Consider another feature of syllogistic reason, of formal logic. Remember, I said if we want to measure, our categories are "all," "none," and "some," and "some" admits of no degrees. It makes no difference if it is one percent, 99 percent, or anywhere in between. How often is that the case? Again, it is not very often.

Most of the time when we are not dealing with universals, it is very important to know matters of degree; for example, whether something is highly probable or whether it is just an unlikely possibility. One criticism would say, "Look, we have picked the model that does not describe in any way the reasoning in which we actually engage." Another and somewhat related criticism is to suggest that most argumentation and most reasoning is not represented well by a form in which the conclusion contains no new information. What we want to do most of the time when we reason is precisely to get from something we already know to something that we do not. We want new information. We want to move from premises that we are fairly confident of, and see if they can lead us to a new conclusion in which we can have confidence. This movement involves a leap of faith, which an arguer tries to justify for us and say, "You ought to make that leap. You ought to make that inference. You ought to derive that conclusion on the basis of those premises." So, what these critiques have suggested is that if we think about mathematical, symbolic, or formal logic as models for reasoning in general, we are going to be led down the wrong path. The model does not represent the kind of reasoning, the kind of arguing, in which we customarily engage.

However, if formal reasoning is not the model, then what is it? From this point of view, it is a highly specialized application of what are much broader general principles of reasoning. The trick that we have played on ourselves for 300 years, this critique would suggest, is to take a highly specialized example as though it were the model case. Why, then, should we study formal reasoning? Why do I devote a lecture to it? Partly to understand how it is used in the areas to which it does apply, and partly because some of the thought patterns of formal logic and some of the errors in formal reasoning are also found in everyday argumentation, as we will see in later lectures. But, what I am really saying here is, let's re-contextualize formal reasoning as a specialized case—a case that is appropriate to mathematics and certain symbolic realms—but let's quit thinking about it as a generalizable model.

Where do we find our generalizable model then? Increasingly, scholars have said we ought to look not to formal reasoning, but to informal reasoning, which deals with structures that are not, and do not, aspire to be certain. In informal reasoning, the argument cannot be extracted from the language in which it is cast. This is both a blessing and a curse. It means that the study of informal reasoning is messier than the study of formal reasoning.

Consider a claim like this one: "If we allow stem-cell research, we are playing God." We could go on and affirm or deny the antecedent and the consequent. If you took a statement like that and put it in the "if, then" structure of formal logic, you could do it, but you would lose so much of what the content of this argument is about. Playing God is not just the equivalent of a P or a Q, an A or B, or any symbol because it has connotations—value judgments of what is permissible and not permissible—and these are bound up in the language itself. We would not reach a conclusion that says we approve of playing God. As we use the language, we would see that as an inconsistent possibility. Playing God is not something that is given to human beings to do, and to say that one is trying to do that is a powerful accusation. It is not a neutral statement. Likewise, neither is the verb "allow" in "If we allow stem-cell research." I could have said, "endorse," "encourage," "permit," "condone," or any of a number of other verbs and they all mean something different, because language itself contains levels of meaning and connotation that are also part of the argument. So, unlike formal reasoning, we cannot extract the argument from the language.

Furthermore, in informal reasoning, the conclusion does contain new information not present in the premises. As I have said, we have reasoned precisely in order to get to a new place from the place where we start out. So, for example, if we reach the conclusion that we ought to allow stem-cell research, we would reach it from premises that deal with science and medicine, morality, and judgments about the nature of the stem-cell. From these premises, often, perhaps, through a long and tortured process of reasoning, we might get to the conclusion that we ought to allow stem-cell research; or conversely, that we ought not to. We get to a conclusion that contains new information; it is not where we started out. The purpose of our reasoning is precisely to get there. As a result, this conclusion does not follow with certainty. Our premises about morality and science might be right, and it still might be the case that we ought not to allow stem-cell research; or conversely, that we should, depending on which way we were making the argument. The conclusion only follows with some degree of probability, and it is important to have some sense of how great that probability is. We are not satisfied with just saying "some." We want to know whether there is an offhand chance that we could be right—whether it is a medium range probability or whether it is highly likely that we could be right.

To recapitulate, informal reasoning cannot be extracted from language. The conclusion does contain new information, and the conclusion follows not with certainty, but only with some degree of probability. We might ask ourselves, "Why should we accept a conclusion that relies on probability? Why should we accept a conclusion that might be wrong?" Well, in brief, the answer is that if the reasoning follows accepted conventions, or a pattern that has been used repeatedly over time and has led to generally good results, we can be fairly confident that it is right. Accumulated experience has borne out that it will usually be right, though not always. What those conventions of formal reasoning are, we will see in more detail several lectures down the road. But, if the question is, "Why should we accept a conclusion that relies on probability?" we should do it because of accumulated experience and because absolute certainty is not possible.

Formal reasoning has its place, but informal reasoning is at the center of argumentation. This approach to reasoning has a long and rich history, going back about 2,500 years, as we will see in the next lecture.

Lecture Four
History of Argumentation Studies

Scope:

The study of informal argumentation can be traced back to the beginnings of rhetoric in ancient Greece. To help citizens defend themselves in court, the Sophists taught techniques of argument. They were accused of divorcing technique from goals. Plato thought that this separation was an inherent difficulty, but Aristotle offered a systematic treatment that showed that the subject was worthy of study. During the early Renaissance, the subject matter of rhetoric was divided, with argumentation assigned to philosophy. The Cartesian method of reasoning, however, left little space for argumentation. Formal logic was held to be the highest form of reasoning, and argumentation tried to imitate it. Since the mid-20th century, though, theorists from different perspectives have identified weaknesses in the formal-logic model and have revitalized the study of argumentation.

Outline

I. Studies of argumentation trace their origins to classical Greece.

    A. The immediate impetus was political.

        1. A tyrant, Thrasybulus of Syracuse, had been overthrown.

        2. Citizens needed to know how to argue in court to recover property that had been seized by the tyrannical regime.

    B. To meet this need, itinerant teachers began to lecture in Athens and the surrounding area.

        1. They were known as Sophists—and that was not a term of derision.

        2. One of the earliest Sophists was Protagoras, known as the "father of debate" because he taught that there were two sides to every question.

        3. Other prominent Sophists included Gorgias and Isocrates.

4. The Sophists introduced the notion of commonplaces, mental storehouses where the materials of argument could be found.
5. The Sophists were accused of excessive concern for technique.
6. It was charged that they regarded winning an argument as an end in itself, regardless of one's purpose or the soundness of one's position.
7. Plato regarded these excesses as inherent in rhetoric (and hence in argumentation) itself.

C. Aristotle offered a systematic treatment of argumentation and rhetoric to demonstrate that the subject was legitimate and worth studying.

D. Argumentation was the foundation of rhetoric, the basis for attempts to influence others.

II. With only minor adjustments, the Aristotelian synthesis continued to dominate the study of argumentation during the Roman era and the medieval period.

A. Romans adapted the theory of the Greeks for pedagogical purposes.
1. Rhetoric was seen as a means of instruction.
2. The subject was divided into invention, arrangement, style, memory, and delivery, with argumentation closely identified with the first two of these canons.
3. Rhetoric was one of the seven liberal arts, and it focused on the training of the citizen-orator.

B. In the medieval period, the dominant social institution was the church, so rhetoric came to be regarded as the study of preaching.

III. Significant redirections of the subject occurred during the early Renaissance.

A. Peter Ramus bifurcated the canons, associating invention and arrangement with philosophy.
1. Rhetorical scholars lost interest in argumentation.
2. They instead developed elaborate systems for classifying figures of speech, gesture, and other stylistic devices.

B. René Descartes developed the method of systematic doubt, maintaining that one could reason only from self-evident premises.

C. These influences remained dominant for approximately 300 years.

    1. Reasoning became identified with the study of formal logic.

    2. Nonformal reasoning sought to emulate the certainty of formal logic.

    3. Within specialized fields, practitioners developed models of reasoning that were claimed to be deductive.

    4. Argumentation was seen, for the most part, as the demonstration of self-evident truth.

D. This trend reached its apex in the early 20th century, with the dominance of logical positivism in philosophy.

IV. During the 20th century, growing awareness of what these approaches omitted led to dissatisfaction with the models of reasoning.

    A. Positivism dismissed, to the realm of meaninglessness, attempts to make sense of some of the perplexities of modern life.

        1. It regarded statements of value as merely reports on the state of one's glands.

        2. It could not establish, for instance, that freedom was better than tyranny or that democracy was better than communism, because it excluded questions of this type from consideration.

    B. The formal deductive model led to two "modern dogmas."

        1. One was the dogma of scientism, holding that nonscientific claims, because they could not be verified, were nonsense and all of equal value.

        2. One was the dogma of irrationalism, holding that nonformal questions could be decided only by irrational means such as force.

    C. Unhappiness with these alternatives led to reformulations of the concepts of reason and rationality and likewise led to a revived role for rhetoric in the study of argumentation.

V. Several intellectual influences of the past 50 years have encouraged this revival of interest.

    A. Toulmin's attempt to explain ethical reasoning led to a more widely applicable model of nonformal reasoning.

    B. Perelman's attempt to explain how people reason about justice led him to the revival of a rhetorical theory based on argumentation.

    C. Hamblin's challenge to the conventional wisdom regarding fallacies fueled the contemporary informal logic movement.

    D. Van Eemeren and Grootendorst examined the role of argumentation in critical discussions, and others interested in "dialogue logics" charted how argumentation occurs in informal settings.

    E. Habermas and other social theorists emphasized the role of communication in the constitution of society and offered normative standards for argumentation under ideal speech conditions.

    F. The "rhetorical turn" in specialized fields of study undermined deductive models and re-established an active role for argument in shaping perception.

VI. Today, argumentation is an exciting and vibrant field of study.

    A. Though solidly grounded in a renewed understanding of rhetoric, it also has strong interdisciplinary appeal.

    B. Breadth and interdisciplinarity have both positive and negative attributes.

    C. The subject has both macro- and micro-levels and both product and process dimensions.

Essential Reading:

"Classical Rhetoric," in Thomas O. Sloane, ed., *Encyclopedia of Rhetoric*, pp. 92–115.

J. Robert Cox and Charles Arthur Willard, eds., *Advances in Argumentation Theory and Research*, pp. xiii–xlvii.

Supplementary Reading:

Michael A. Gilbert, *Coalescent Argumentation*, chapter 1.

Frans H. van Eemeren et al., *Fundamentals of Argumentation Theory,* chapter 2.

Questions to Consider:

1. What might be some of the key trends in argumentation theory if Peter Ramus had not moved the subject from rhetoric to philosophy?

2. What are the similarities and differences between current approaches to persuasion and those that were dominant in classical Greece?

Lecture Four—Transcript
History of Argumentation Studies

In the last lecture, we attempted to distinguish argumentation in general, which is our concern, from formal reasoning, which is a specialized application of it. I suggested that general argumentation grounded in informal reasoning had a very long history. Now, I want, with all immodesty, to survey 25 centuries of history and explore how this field of study developed and how it came to take the shape it has today.

We start off in ancient Greece in the 5th century B.C. This is usually regarded as the period of time in which the study of rhetoric and argumentation began. The immediate impulse for it was, frankly, political. There had been a tyrant named Thrasybulus of Syracuse, who had been overthrown, and a democratic regime was established. This created a very practical political need. During the period of tyrannical rule, private property had been seized, had been expropriated, and citizens now needed to go to court and to make arguments on their behalf with regard to the title of their property. They needed to know how to do it. There were not professional lawyers then; citizens represented themselves in court. They needed to know how to justify the claim that a piece of property that they said was theirs really was theirs. In response to this need, a class of people developed—we call them professionals today—who were teachers. They were itinerant teachers who went around from place to place and lectured in Athens and in the surrounding area to teach people the skills to argue their claims in court. These people were called Sophists. Now, again, this is a term that has negative connotations today. Sophistry is talked about as empty appeals that do not really have any significant substance to them; but at that time the Sophists were highly respected.

One of the earliest of the Sophists was a man named Protagoras, whom we remember as the "Father of debate" because he taught that there were always at least two sides to every question. Hence, the outcome of the question was not given or self-evident, but was relative to the arguments that were advanced for it. So, Protagoras introduced the very kind of mindset that we talked about in the last lecture. Among the other leading Sophists were Gorgias, who focused on different styles of language in argument, and Isocrates—not to be confused with Socrates—who emphasized the role of probabilities, and who, by the way, was one of the leading opponents of Plato. Isocrates and Plato sort of represented the two poles of antiquity: Plato defending philosophy; Isocrates defending rhetoric. Plato was seeking certainty; Isocrates was emphasizing probability. Plato was the man of contemplation and reflection; Isocrates was the man of action; and so on.

The Sophists introduced the notion that there were, if you will, storehouses in the mind, or commonplaces to which one could go to find the themes or the appeals to use in the arguments to be made in court. Also, they suggested that there were a finite number of these places in the mind. So, if you could learn these commonplaces, you would have a storehouse of resources to use in making the claims that you would need to make.

There is one other thing, by the way, that the Sophists did, and I always admired them for it, and that was that they introduced the principle that teachers should be paid. But, they came to be criticized and no one criticized them more vigorously than Plato. The essence of Plato's criticism of the Sophists was that they regarded winning the case as an end in itself, regardless of one's purpose or the soundness of one's position—just as we sometimes stereotype argumentation today. The charge that would be made against the Sophists is that they made the weaker appear to be the stronger case. They made the worse appear to be the better case. How did they do that? The charge was that they did it by being so concerned by technique, as an end in itself, apart from the substance of the matter, and apart from what was right. So, they would teach people with weak positions how to make them seem stronger than they really were. Of course, the assumption underlying this charge by Plato against the Sophists was that there was a priori. There was some notion of what was right and what was wrong—what was worse and what was better, what was weaker and what was stronger—that you could determine these features of a case apart from making the arguments for it, assuming that all these things could be known and applied. Plato thought that the excessive concern of the Sophists for technique was inherent in the subject of rhetoric and argument itself; so he derided the study and practice of argumentation.

Indeed, there is an interpretation of one of Plato's most famous dialogues, *Phaedrus*, which suggests that what Plato does in that dialogue is to establish the requirements for good rhetoric, such that they could not possibly be met. In order to practice good rhetoric, one must know the nature of the soul and all the different kinds of souls, and so on and so forth. These were requirements that could not possibly be met, and so by this interpretation, *Phaedrus* is, in large part, an attack on rhetoric. It suggests that if you employ rhetoric, or argument; that if you believe, as Protagoras did, that there are two sides to every question and the outcome is relative to argument, you are just focusing on appearances, not on realities. It is focusing on what is fleeting and ephemeral, not on what is enduring and timeless. Of course, Plato was concerned with the latter. So, we have, all the way back in antiquity, this opposition between rhetoric and philosophy, appearance and reality, probability and truth, by Isocrates and Plato.

It fell on Aristotle to try to develop a synthesis of these positions. Aristotle argued that rhetoric and argument were neither moral nor immoral instruments. They were instruments; they could be used for good or evil. But, argumentation was a skill. It was a practical art. Aristotle wrote a book called *Rhetoric*—which is still studied widely today—in which he tried to set out this view. It is in that book that he offered the definition that I mentioned a few lectures back, when he said that rhetoric was the faculty or skill of discovering the available means of persuasion in the given case. That view led Aristotle to an emphasis on audience analysis, to a view on the kinds of appeals that one could use, and the circumstances under which they would be appropriate or inappropriate.

Aristotle's *Rhetoric* is sometimes thought of almost as a recipe book because it suggests all these different possibilities that an orator could use. The larger purpose that Aristotle had in mind was to try to resolve this split between Isocrates and Plato. It was to suggest that the study of rhetoric was legitimate and worth knowing about, and argumentation was the foundation of it; thus, it was a skill that ought to be taught so that it could be put to good and useful purposes. Aristotle really represents the synthesis of classic Greek approaches to argumentation and rhetoric. This synthesis, with only minor adjustments, continued to dominate the study of rhetoric, not only through the rest of classical Greece, but through the Roman Era and into the Medieval Period, as well.

The Romans took the theories of rhetoric developed by the Greeks, particularly by Aristotle, and adapted them largely for pedagogical purposes. So, the Romans saw rhetoric as a means of instruction; and if you will, argument and rhetoric became a sort of early theory of teaching. How do we teach? How do we instruct students? How do people learn?

The Romans took the concepts that, especially, Aristotle had articulated, and systematized them. They did that by dividing the study of rhetoric into five parts, which they called canons. The canons were invention, arrangement, style, memory, and delivery. Invention was the process of discovery, of finding what could be used in an argument and selecting what would be used. Invention was the process of going through the storehouses of the mind, identifying the available resources, and then choosing them from among them. Arrangement, as its name suggests, refers to organization. Indeed, the earliest work on patterns of organization came from the Romans. They talked about the different parts of a speech, what should be done in each part, and how the parts should work together for persuasive purposes. Style focused on the use of language, how different kinds of language could suggest a different level or tone, and how particular words or phrases could be chosen. Memory referred to the process of keeping in mind what one was about to say, and it led, ultimately, to the discovery and study of all sorts of mnemonic devices—devices to aid the memory. It did not necessarily mean memorization, but it referred to keeping in one's mind the elements of the appeal. Delivery referred to the physical presentation,—the use of the voice, body, gesture, and so on. So, rhetoric was neatly divided up into these five parts and, as you could imagine, the first two of them—invention and arrangement—were most closely linked to argumentation. Argumentation became the process of identifying the appeals that one could use, and figuring out how to put them together in an order or structure.

It was also the Romans, as you probably remember, who organized whole fields of study and developed the original seven liberal arts. Rhetoric was one of these; it was put together with logic and grammar. The three—logic, grammar, and rhetoric—were called the Trivium—not be confused with "trivial." The Trivium were the fields that were seen as essential to the training of the good citizen orator. The ultimate objective of the Roman educational system was to train people to be, in Quintilian's words, "the good person speaking well," because that is what the job of the citizen was seen as being—being able to speak effectively and to influence others through argument.

This view, by the way, held through much of the Medieval Period, as well. The canons that were associated with the Romans, and especially with Cicero, were maintained. The one significant change was that if education was the dominant influence of the Romans' use of rhetoric, for much of the Medieval Era, it was religion. Religion was the dominant social institution, so rhetoric and argument came to be seen as a theory of preaching. This theory, once again, relied on the same canons that the Romans developed; that, in turn, was a systematization of a whole way of thought that went back to classical Greece.

Now, I want to jump all the way to the 16th century or so—the early Renaissance. It was then that some significant changes occurred in the way people thought about the study of rhetoric and argumentation. There was an otherwise relatively obscure philosopher by the name of Peter Ramus who took the five canons of the Romans and split them into two groups: invention and arrangement on the one hand; style, memory, and delivery on the other. Ramus took invention and arrangement, and he lifted them from rhetoric and assigned them to philosophy, because these were seen as part of a discovery process of figuring out what was true. Rhetoric was left with style, memory, and delivery, which some people would regard as the least intellectual elements of the subject and, certainly, the least relevant to argumentation.

But, notice what Ramus's division implied. It implied that the process of discovering what was true was separate from the process of presenting it after it had been discovered. Remember, Aristotle had linked the two together. He regarded all of his subject matter as interrelated. But, under the influence of Ramus, discovery of truth was distinguished from the presentation of truth. Rhetoric was seen, not as a matter of making and justifying claims with an audience in mind—not as argumentation—but as a way of giving effective presentation to what philosophy had already determined to be correct. This was a view that would have a profound influence over the study of rhetoric for the next couple of centuries, removing it ever further from the kinds of concerns we have been talking about and focusing it much more on mechanics.

What did scholars of rhetoric do during this time? They developed elaborate manuals, lists, and category systems of figures of speech, ways of gesture, ways to move the head and to position the body. There were whole books published with hundreds of diagrams of different gestures, suggesting different kinds of things on how to use the body during delivery of a speech. That is what rhetoric was, while philosophy took over invention and arrangement.

But then, something significant happened within the field of philosophy, particularly under the influence of René Descartes. We remember Descartes probably most of all for his statement, "I think, therefore I am." What we forget is that what that statement is, is an answer to the question, "What can you know?" Descartes believed that we ought to systematically doubt everything, and we ought to accept as true only what could be shown to be self-evident. What was self-evident? "If I think, therefore I exist." The Cartesian revolution in philosophy, as it is sometimes called, was marked by this quest for certainty, for self-evidence.

Guess what happens to those borrowed canons from rhetoric, invention and arrangement? Once philosophy takes on a concern with certainty and self-evidence, they whither away. Indeed, for much of the 17th, 18th, and into the 19th century, there is little further advance in the understanding of these important canons and hence, little advance of argumentation. Reasoning becomes identified with the study of formal logic alone, because it yields certainty. This is when formal logic began to be seen as the model of all reasoning. But, what is not formal should aspire to the standards of formal logic; it should be taken as the goal. Within specialized fields of study, practitioners develop models of reasoning that were claimed to be deductive or certain, or at least to approach that goal.

What was argumentation? Very simply, it was the demonstration of self-evident truth. What would be the model case of argumentation in such a view? Geometrical proofs. You probably remember studying geometry where you make a statement, and then you make a reason for it on a table of statements and reasons until you end up with a certain conclusion. That is what argumentation was thought to be under the influence of Descartes—a demonstration of self-evident truth. This point of view had a tremendous influence, even into the 20th century. In fact, some people have suggested that the very apex of this view was an early 20th century movement known as Logical

Positivism, which was predominant in the years immediately following World War I. While I oversimplify what Logical Positivism was, I do not think it is unfair to say that it held that only words that clearly stand for something are meaningful. Hence, that a large amount of the language that we use does not have any referent and, therefore, does not have any meaning. The rich connotations of language did not count because they were not about anything, just a report of our feelings. Now, we come to the 20th century.

Over the course of the last century, there has been a growing awareness of what this whole approach of Cartesianism leaves out. I think it is fair to say that dissatisfaction with the approach has led to rethinking an old idea of formal reasoning as the goal and Cartesian philosophy as the model. What did this approach do? It dismissed to the realm of meaninglessness attempts to make sense of the perplexities of modern life.

For example, it regarded statements of value—"Peace is good," "Democracy is good," "This piece of art is beautiful"—as nothing more than reports, if you will, on the state of our glands. When I say, "Democracy is good," what I am simply saying is, "I like it." I'm not making any claim on you, because I cannot. I have no way to defend the claim with any certainty. So, statements of value are meaningless. Statements about what ought to be done are meaningless. So, for example, it was suggested that one could not establish that freedom was better than tyranny, or that Democracy was better than Communism, or the reverse, because Logical Positivism excluded from consideration questions of this type.

The literary critic and theorist Wayne Booth has suggested that this whole view has led to what he termed "two modern dogmas." Of course, his use of the term dogma is no accident. In a kind of ironic, if not perverse, reversal, our emphasis on certainty and reasoning leads us to accept some things as dogmatic matters of faith. One of those dogmas he called Scientism, by which he meant the belief that non-scientific claims were all of equal value because there was no way to verify them, deduce them, or know them with certainty. So one was as good as another—"I like Democracy, you like Totalitarianism—equally well." The other dogma he labeled Irrationalism. That was the belief that things that could not be decided with certainty, but could only be decided by whim or by force; that the stronger would prevail. The emphasis was on the act of will.

Now, I don't know about you, but I find these dogmas, Scientism and Irrationalism, unacceptable. I am not prepared to say that non-scientific claims are of equal value, or that matters that are uncertain could be settled only by force. Increasingly, during the 20th century, people reflected on these dogmas and came to the same conclusion. But what is the alternative to accepting? Go back to the beginning and question the Cartesian assumption that certainty is what we are after. Go back to the beginning and question the assumption that invention and arrangement are matters of philosophy, rather than rhetoric. Go back to the beginning and revive a classical understanding of what argumentation is all about. There have been several intellectual influences over the past 50 or 60 years that have done just that. Interestingly, they have come from different parts of the world and different fields of study. I want to mention several of these, without going into detail, so that we get a sense of what has happened as people began to question the idea that Cartesianism, Logical Positivism, and the quest for certainty were our models.

There is a contemporary English philosopher—although he is now living in America—Stephen Toulmin, who set out to answer this question in the 1950s: When people talk about ethics, how do they reason? You see, he rejects the notion that we don't reason. He rejects the notion that ethical discussions are nonsense, or just reports of the state of our glands. He starts from the ground up and he asks, how do people reason when they talk about ethics? He ended up developing a model of reason, which we will say more about in the next lecture, that he believes better accounts for what we do than does formal logic or a quest for certainty.

Meanwhile, from a completely different perspective, a Belgian philosopher of jurisprudence named Chaim Perelman asked this question: When people talk about justice, how do they reason? Notice, again, he rejects the notion that we don't reason; rejects the notion that it is meaningless. He asks, when people talk about justice, when they talk about what courts ought to do, how do they reason? He ended up developing a whole theory that, more than anything else, went all the way back to classical rhetoric. So the way people reason, he says, is they make claims seeking the adherence of audiences. They speak to a particular audience, but they also have in mind a larger, ultimate universal audience, which provides the norms and standards for how they argue. He wrote a very long book explaining how people do that, and the different methods and resources they use.

In Australia, a philosopher, Charles Hamblin, took the idea of fallacies, which of course comes from formal logic—fallacies are formally incorrect arguments, at least in their traditional understanding—and he said, in effect, "Wait a minute, let's explore some of these fallacies!" Depending on how people use them and in what context, they may not be fallacious at all! They may be perfectly good arguments. What results in our calling them fallacies is the mistaken assumption that we ought to be guided by this model of formal reasoning seeking certainty.

In the Netherlands, two scholars, Frans van Eemeren and Rob Grootendorst, have done a whole series of others asking this question: When people engage in conversation in trying to resolve problems, how do the conversations proceed and how should they? Van Eemeren, Grootendorst, and their colleagues have worked out a whole logic of conversation for critical discussions, which they have called Pragma-Dialectics. Notice what that term Pragma-Dialectics does. It goes back to the concept of dialectic, which we explored in the first lecture, in an interchange of questions and answers; it realizes that this is taking place for a pragmatic purpose—resolving problems by influencing other people as to what the outcome should be. Their work, within the realm of conversational-analysis, goes back to this old notion of dialectic and rhetoric in relationship.

A contemporary German scholar Jürgen Habermas and other theorists of society have focused on the role of communication in making a society, and they have offered normative standards for how arguments should proceed under ideal social conditions. That is, it should not be influenced by force. Conversations should not end arbitrarily. The force of the better argument should prevail, and so on. These have become normative standards against which Habermas and other critics have measured actual practice.

In the United States, within several different fields of study in the social sciences and the humanities, there has been a new role of discourse and interpretation in understanding, which rejects the notion that understanding is given and self-evident. Now, all these different trends, while they come from very different routes, have worked to revive the classical understanding of argumentation, grounded in rhetoric and dialectic, as well as logic. Today, it is, again, a vibrant field of study.

After these first four lectures, we have now completed our study of the intellectual and historical backgrounds of argumentation. It is time now to investigate what arguments look like, how they arise in controversies, and how controversy is perceived. We will start there next time.

Lecture Five
Argument Analysis and Diagramming

Scope:

This lecture examines how controversies begin and how the process of arguing produces individual arguments. It will consider the claim as the most basic part of the argument and will identify different types of claims. Then it will present the basic structure of an individual argument, consisting of a claim, evidence for it, an inference linking the evidence to the claim, and a warrant justifying that inference. These components are not always apparent in actual arguments, but they can be extracted and diagrammed for purposes of argument analysis and appraisal.

Outline

I. People argue—that is, they engage in reason giving—when certain conditions are met.

    A. Some controversy or disagreement exists between them.

    B. The controversy is nontrivial.

    C. The assent of the other party is desired; therefore, one cannot simply abandon the situation.

    D. Assent is desired only if it is freely given.

        1. Respect for the other party makes this criterion essential.

        2. Our desire for confidence in the result also requires this condition.

    E. No easier means exists for resolving the disagreement.

        1. We cannot use empirical methods.

        2. We cannot consult a universally recognized authority.

        3. We cannot deduce the answer with certainty from what we already know.

    F. In short, we argue about significant controversies that are inherently uncertain; we argue about that which could be otherwise.

II. How do controversies begin?

    A. We can consider some sample statements that might be made in conversation.

1. In August 2005, George W. Bush was president of the United States.
2. The Teaching Company sells this course for $49.95.
3. The red tie is prettier than the blue one.
4. The city government is unsatisfactory.
5. Capital punishment is murder.
6. Congress ought to pass the President's budget.

B. With respect to each of these statements, how would we know which ones were true?
1. In some cases, as in statement 1, we could rely on common knowledge.
2. In some cases, as in statement 2, we could rely on widely shared empirical methods.
3. In some cases, as in statement 3, we could rely on personal judgment or taste.
4. In some cases, as in statements 4–6, further discussion would be required.

C. The knowledge, method, or judgment relied on will determine what sort of response one is likely to make to each of the six statements.
1. The response may be nonargumentative, such as silence or immediate assent or denial.
2. Nonargumentative responses will occur when the matter is trivial, there is a wide consensus, or the subject is so emotionally intense that discussion is not possible.
3. Statements 1–3 would probably trigger nonargumentative responses, in which case the controversy would end.

D. If the response is "How do you know?" or "What do you mean?", the maker of the statement must supply reasons that will be assessed and responded to further.
1. If the reasons are deemed satisfactory, the argument then will stop.
2. If not, the arguer will need to elaborate further on the reasons or introduce additional reasons to satisfy the objections.
3. This situation will be especially likely to occur when previously accepted assumptions are challenged or when new situations present themselves.

E. When one speaks or writes in public, rather than engages in conversation, one acts as if such a challenge has occurred, and thus that there is a need to defend one's claims.

    1. Claims are the statements that the listener is asked to accept, for which the speaker will provide reasons if needed; there are four basic types of claims.

    2. Claims of fact involve description.

        a. They concern matters that, in theory, can be described and verified independently by others.

        b. They may relate to the past, present, or future.

    3. Claims of definition involve interpretation.

        a. They place concepts in categories and provide perspective.

        b. This interpretation is important because definitions are not neutral.

    4. Claims of value involve judgment.

        a. Judgment represents an appraisal or evaluation.

        b. The evaluation can be absolute or comparative.

        c. It can involve instrumental or terminal values.

    5. Claims of policy involve action.

        a. They are assertions about what should be done.

        b. They are characteristic of deliberative bodies, such as Congress.

    6. Classifying claims is important because the proof requirements differ for different types of claims.

F. It is important to understand the components of an argument, in addition to the claim.

    1. Not all these components may be stated explicitly, but they are implicit in the argument and can be filled in by the analyst.

    2. An advocate advances a claim, which may or may not be accepted immediately.

        a. If it is, the matter ends, and there is no further argument.

        b. If it is not, then the advocate will need to produce evidence to support the claim.

    3. If the evidence is not immediately accepted, then one of two things will happen.

        a. If the truth of the evidence is in dispute, then a separate argument will be advanced to establish it.

      b. If the truth of the evidence is accepted but it is not seen as justifying the claim, then a warrant is provided for the inference from evidence to claim.
  4. If the warrant is not accepted, then there will be a separate argument to back it up.
  5. Exceptions may be noted, and the claim may need to be qualified.
  6. This process continues until the arguers reach agreement, or the dispute is resolved by a third party.

G. We have identified the major components in a model of argument adapted from the writing of the contemporary philosopher Stephen Toulmin.
  1. Claims are the statements that we want listeners to believe and on which we want them to act.
  2. Evidence represents the grounds for making a claim.
      a. It is not identical to the claim but is used to support it.
      b. It must be accepted by the audience, or a separate argument will be required to establish its truth.
  3. The inference is the main proof line leading from evidence to claim.
  4. The warrant is a license to make the inference.
      a. Like the evidence, it either must be accepted by the audience, or else it must be established by separate argument.
      b. It is a general rule that recognizes the possibility of exceptions.
      c. Exceptions to the warrant require qualifying the claim.
  5. An example will illustrate how this model captures the essential components of an argument.

Essential Reading:

"Controversy," in Thomas O. Sloane, ed., *Encyclopedia of Rhetoric*, pp. 169–171.

Frans H. van Eemeren, et al., *Fundamentals of Argumentation Theory: A Handbook of Historical Backgrounds and Contemporary Developments*, pp. 129–149.

Supplementary Reading:

Richard D. Rieke and Malcolm O. Sillars, *Argumentation and Critical Decision Making*, pp. 107–111.

Stephen Toulmin, *The Uses of Argument*, pp. 94–145.

Dale Hample, "The Toulmin Model and the Syllogism," in William L. Benoit, Dale Hample, and Pamela J. Benoit, eds., *Readings in Argumentation*, pp. 225–238.

Questions to Consider:

1. How are productive controversies different from those that are merely contentious and quarrelsome?

2. How does the diagram of argument make clear that disagreements must be built on some level of agreement?

Simple Argument

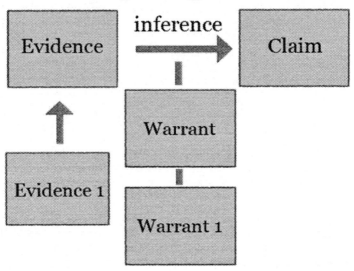

Argument Example

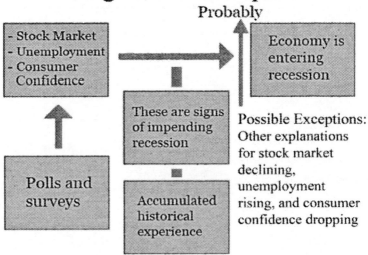

Lecture Five—Transcript
Argument Analysis and Diagramming

In the first four lectures, we have explored the nature of argumentation and some of the points of view that are implied or assumed in studying this field. We have examined how formal and informal reasoning differ, and we have traced the development of argumentation studies across 2,500 years of history. Now we begin a series of lectures on argumentation's strategies and tactics. We start by considering where we find arguments and what they look like.

What does it take to get people to argue? Basically, five preconditions must be met, and from the discussions we have already had, these should be fairly obvious. So, let me tick them off briefly. First, there is a disagreement or controversy between people. Second, the disagreement matters to the people who are in it; it is not neutral or trivial. Third, the assent of the other party is desired. But, fourth: assent is valued only if it is freely given. Finally, fifth: there is no easier or less risky way to resolve the disagreement. We can remember those things from the discussions we have already had. When those five conditions are satisfied, people will argue.

How does a controversy begin? Well, let's consider some examples. Let's consider six different claims that we might imagine somebody making. First: In August 2005, George W. Bush was president of the United States. Second: The Teaching Company sells this course for $49.95. Third: The red tie is prettier than the blue one. Fourth: The city government is unsatisfactory. Fifth: Capital punishment is murder. Finally, sixth: Congress ought to pass the President's budget. Now, these are somewhat different kinds of statements; some of them, as claims, will be more likely to produce arguments than others.

Think for a minute about this question: With respect to each of these statements, how would you know whether you should believe it? Well, let's try. Look at statement one: In August 2005, George W. Bush was president of the United States. That is an item of common knowledge. It is easily verified so we can say, "Everyone knows that," and that would probably be the end of the matter. It is not likely—unless we have imagined the time a hundred years from now, perhaps—that people would dispute the claim that George W. Bush was president of the United States.

Sometimes we can rely, not on common knowledge, but on widely shared empirical methods. Look at statement two: The Teaching Company sells this course for $49.95. There is an easy way to find out whether you should believe that. Go to their catalog and look it up in their price list. (By the way, I hope you find that it sells for a lot more than $49.95 because this course is worth every penny.) But there is an easy way to find out the answer and one probably would not argue about it at any length.

Sometimes we decide whether or not to not believe a claim, regarding it simply as a matter of taste. Look at statement three: The red tie is prettier than the blue one. How do you know? Well, I just like it better. It is probably the end of the matter if I say that; or if I say that red is my favorite color; or, "I've never liked blue," or something like that. These are just matters of taste, and that is probably as far as the conversation would go.

But now look at statements four, five, and six. They are quite different. With each of those statements I could easily imagine someone making the statement and someone else saying, "What do you mean by that? How do you know? What do you have to go on?" or something like that. In cases like those, further discussion will be required. Then, the person who made the statement has to come up with some reasons for it. Statement four: The city government is unsatisfactory. Why do you say that? Well, they won't even plow the streets when it snows. That is a reason to support the claim. Look at statement five: Capital punishment is murder. What makes you think so? Well, it is killing people, isn't it? Or look at statement six: Congress ought to pass the president's budget. Why? Because it is a good budget and it has the right kind of priorities.

Now, look what happened with statements four, five, and six. In each case, the statement was questioned and the person who made the statement then had to come up with some sort of reason that you ought to believe the statement. The other person might find the reason perfectly adequate. I say, "The city government is unsatisfactory." You say, "Why?" I say, "Because they won't even plow the streets when it snows." You say, "Yes, you are right about that," and that is the end of the matter. I have come up with a reason. You have said, in effect, that the reason justifies the claim I made. You will reach the claim; you will travel with me to the claim. You will agree to it on the basis of the reason that I have provided.

However, sometimes the reason won't be deemed satisfactory. "Capital punishment is murder." "How do you know?" "Well, it is killing people, isn't it?" "Yes, but that is just a play on words. There is killing and then there is killing. It makes a difference if it is sanctioned by the state," and so on and so forth. We could imagine that this argument might proceed on out for a while. If the original reasons are not satisfactory, then the arguer will need to elaborate those reasons further or to come up with new ones, and the process continues. It continues until the parties to the argument conclude that they have a set of reasons that justify the claims that have been advanced. In the case of really controversial questions, this argument might continue for quite a long time. There are arguments that have gone on for centuries.

In any case, however, the first building block of an argument is the claim—the statement that readers or listeners are asked to accept. Most theorists of argument recognize four different types of claims. The differences can be important because different types of claims usually have different proof requirements. How you go about justifying the claim will depend on what kind of claim it is. The four basic types of claims are fact, definition, value, and policy. Let me say just a bit about each.

I start with claims of fact. These involve description. They concern matters that, at least in theory, could be described and verified independently of the arguers; they are matters about which, in theory, they would have a high degree of consensus once they are verified. Now, I say, "in theory," because often there is really not a way to stop the argument and verify the matter independently. Consider this example: Al Gore received more popular votes than George W. Bush in the 2000 election. This is a matter that, in theory, could be verified independently. You could look it up in the almanac. But, of course, if there is one thing we know from the election of 2000, is that it is not that clear. What counts as a vote? What got counted as a vote? What were the error rates? If all of those things were sorted out, it would perhaps be controversial whether Bush or Gore received the greater number of popular votes. But, that is still a claim of fact.

Claims of definition deal with meaning or interpretation. We might think that those are not really matters to argue about either. After all, if you want to know the definition of a word, look it up. But, that is a simpleminded notion of definitions and it assumes that definitions are neutral. Think about one of the statements in our list: "Capital punishment is murder." That is a definitional claim; but murder is not a neutral term. It is a term that, because of its connotations, will evoke disagreement about whether it is appropriate to put capital punishment in that category. So, definitional questions are often very important for the precise reason that definitions are not neutral; they are laden with connotations and implications that can form the basis of a dispute. So, we have fact and definition.

The third kind of claim is value, which involves a judgment of goodness or badness, rightness or wrongness, beauty or ugliness, and so on. A judgment represents an evaluation, an appraisal, according to some kind of standards or criteria. Sometimes the appraisal is absolute; for example, one of the statements we used before, "The city government is unsatisfactory." It is an absolute judgment; it is "unsatisfactory." Sometimes claims of value are comparative; for example, "Economic growth is more important than environmental protection." Claims of value can be about terminal values—that is, things that are good and bad in themselves; or they can involve instrumental values—things that are good or bad as they lead to something else.

The final category of claims is policy. These are claims that involve action. If I had to guess, I would guess that there are probably more arguments that occur on policy claims than any other kind because they address the question, "What should we do?" Typically, they contain some form of the word "should" or "ought" in their statement because these are claims about what should take place or what ought to happen. They are characteristic of deliberative bodies, such as Congress or a legislature; but they also characterize informal deliberations between friends whenever people decide what to do. So, "Congress should pass the president's budget" is a policy claim, but so is, "You should change your Internet service provider." They both deal with the question, "What should we do?" So, those are the four types of claims: fact, definition, value, and policy.

Now let's consider what happens when an advocate advances a claim; in the process, we will identify the other parts of an argument, the other building blocks, in addition to the claim. An advocate makes a claim. We can imagine a very simple diagram—a box with the word "claim" in it. That is all there is because that claim may be immediately accepted. For example, a person might say, "We are heading into a recession." The other person might say, "Well, I guess that is right," and that is the end of the matter. The claim is immediately accepted. If that happens, there is no argument, no further discussion.

But if the claim is not immediately accepted, if the other person says, "Why do you say that?" or "How do know?" or "What do you have to go on?" then the original advocate has to produce evidence to support the claim, to give reasons for the claim in the language we have been using so far. So, in that situation, let us imagine that the person who said, "We are heading into a recession," and is asked, "How do you know?" replies, "Well, the stock market is weakening." Now we can imagine a diagram, where over on the left we have a box with the word "evidence" in it, and the evidence in this case is that "the stock market is weakening." So, we have a box for the claim and a box for the evidence, and we have an arrow drawn from the evidence box going over to the box that was labeled "claim." That arrow represents an inference that says that the fact that "the stock market is weakening" should be taken as a reason for the claim that says, "We are heading into a recession." Now, that might be the end of the matter. Once we say, "the stock market is weakening," the other person will accept that the stock market, indeed, is weakening, and that is a reason to think we are heading into a recession. It is a very simple structure of argument with evidence, claim, and an implicit inference linking the two.

Often, that will not be the end of the matter; the evidence and the inference will not be immediately accepted. Then, a couple of things could happen depending on what comes next. If I say, "We are heading into a recession," and you ask, "How do you know?" and I reply, "Because the stock market is weakening," then you might say, "I really don't think so. That does not match what I understand about the stock market. Show me that it is weakening." Now what I have to do is to provide some additional evidence to back up the first piece of evidence. You might think of it by saying, I now have to present a new argument; in what originally was evidence—mainly "that the stock market is weakening"—now becomes the claim. That is what I now have to justify. I do so by introducing some new evidence; that is, "I cite the Dow Jones industrial average going down," or, "the NASDAQ index going down," and so on. We could represent this in a diagram by taking the last one we had with evidence leading to a claim, and now it is the evidence we have to support. So, below the evidence we have another box that I will call "evidence one," and this is the Dow Jones and the NASDAQ figures with an inference leading up to the original evidence box. In other words, I am inferring that the Dow Jones and the NASDAQ indexes are authoritative grounds for believing the stock market is weakening. Because the stock market is weakening, I infer that we are heading into a recession. So I have shored up my original evidence by providing additional evidence. If you did not accept that evidence, I would need still more.

But now, suppose that what is in dispute is not whether "the stock market is weakening," but whether there is any connection between the stock market weakening and a recession. In that case, what you are doing is challenging, not the truth of my evidence, but the link between my evidence and the claim that I have made. You are challenging that arrow that went from evidence to claim. In that situation, I have to defend that it is okay to make that inference. I have to defend that we can travel along that arrow from evidence to claim. That might require me to shore up, or to buttress that arrow. We can represent that by a chart that looks like the second one with the evidence box leading to the claim; except, holding up the arrow, if you will, we will draw a line to another box that we will label "warrant." If you say, "Why does the stock market weakening show that we are heading into a recession?" I have to give you some warrant for making that inference, some warrant that says it is okay to go from here to here. What I might do is say, "Look, weakening in the stock market is generally a sign of an impending recession." I am telling you, in other words, that I am making an inference from sign, that one thing can be taken as a sign, or as a predictor of the other. So now, if you questioned the link between my evidence and my claim, I have given you some basis for accepting that link. I have given you a warrant for it.

Now, what if you question the warrant? What if you say, "I don't understand why we should take the weakening of the stock market as a sign of recession; what reason do you have to think that?" Then, I have to back up the warrant. You might think of it as establishing a new argument in which the original warrant is now the claim, which I have to establish. I have to show you that it is okay to regard a weakening stock market as a sign of a recession. So, we take the diagram that we just looked at, where there is evidence leading to claim; then, we draw a warrant box under the link. We have to back up this warrant, so we will draw another box underneath it—and I will call it "warrant one"—that links to the original warrant. What is warrant one? Well, I might appeal to historical evidence and say, "Historically, most of the time when the stock market drops, it has been a good predictor of a recession. Therefore, we are justified in saying that weakening of the stock market is a sign of an impending recession." So, I have re-established my warrant; with that warrant, I have justified the link that says, "We can take the weakening of the stock market as a reason to conclude that the economy is heading into a recession."

Now, this process that I have been describing, of making claims, offering evidence, having an inference providing warrants, shoring up the evidence and warrants as necessary, continues. It continues until the argument reaches its termination—the arguers reach an agreement, or a third party resolves the result. What we have seen in the course of working with these simple diagrams that I have explained so far is what the basic parts of an argument are. There are four: the claim, the evidence for the claim, the inference that links evidence and claim, and the warrant that authorizes or legitimizes our making that inference—claim, evidence, inference, and warrant.

I want to emphasize that these parts are not always explicit. In fact, it is hard for me to imagine listening to a conversation, or reading a newspaper editorial, or seeing the text of a speech and seeing advocates who explicitly say, "My claim is…," "My evidence is…," "The inference I am making here is…," "The warrant for it is…," "I back up this warrant by saying so and so…," or anything like that. Arguers often leave out the identification of the parts. They may even omit some of the parts because they figure that an audience will assume them, and so they do not need to be mentioned. It doesn't necessarily weaken the argument if some elements are left unstated. But, when we analyze arguments, we reconstruct them, filling in what was implicit, as well as acknowledging what was said explicitly. Then, we can study the argument and assess its quality.

Now, what we have done here is to develop a working model of argument, identifying the components and sketching their relationships. This model is adapted from the work of the contemporary philosopher Stephen Toulmin and, as I have already suggested, it derives ordinary argument better than does the formal syllogism. The claim is the statement we want listeners to believe and act upon. The evidence represents the grounds for making the claim; it is what answers the question, "What do you have to go on?" The inference is the main proof line that links the evidence to the claim. The warrant is a license to make the inference.

Now, notice that both the evidence and the warrant ultimately have to be agreed to and accepted by the audience, or by the other party if you are in a dispute in an informal setting. It has to be agreed to. If not, then there is additional backing provided for it until it is agreed to. This is a graphic demonstration of something I said in another context in an earlier lecture, when I said that argumentation is cooperative and there is agreement underlying every disagreement. If the parties do not agree to the truth of the evidence or to the warrant, then they cannot discuss what the relationship is between these things and the claim.

Sometimes the warrant is not so clear. There may be exceptions to it—it is a general rule—but there are exceptions. When that happens, then the claim has to be qualified or modified, and these exceptions or modifiers are also incorporated into the model.

Let's see how the model works with the argument that we have been discussing. I am now referring to a chart that looks very much like the one with the evidence, the claim, the warrant, and the inference; but this time I have filled in some content, so we can relate it to this argument. The claim we are making is, "The economy is entering a recession." What is the evidence we might offer? First, "The stock market is declining." Second, if we want more evidence, "The unemployment rate is going up." Third, if we want more evidence, "Ratings of consumer confidence are dropping." These are the reasons we have for saying the economy is entering a recession. They are the evidence. We see the arrow that links the evidence to the claim. On the basis of the stock market declining, unemployment rising, and consumer confidence dropping, we say, "The economy is entering into a recession." But remember that we said the evidence might be questioned; and if so, it would need to be backed up with additional evidence. So, just in case, I have put below the evidence box, where I had below evidence one, that we referred to specific polls and surveys that back up the evidence about the stock market, the unemployment rate, and consumer confidence.

Now, what licenses us to make that inference is the warrant, "These things are signs of an impending recession. The stock market drop, unemployment rate, and consumer confidence are signs, or predictors of an impending recession." That is what holds up the inference. But remember, I said the warrant might be questioned, too. So, underneath the warrant box, I referred to the additional warrant we might provide, warrant one, which is accumulated historical experience. Over time, these things—a drop in the stock market, and so on—usually have preceded a recession.

But then, remember, I said this is a general rule; there could be exceptions. So, off to the side of the warrant box, I have put some possible exceptions—unless there are other explanations for the stock market declining or unemployment rising, such as, "The stock market is declining because stocks were overpriced as a result of speculation and now the bubble has burst." "Unemployment is rising because it is seasonal and more people are coming into the labor force." "Consumer confidence is dropping because people are worried about some extraneous things that are going on." These might be exceptions; or they might be countervailing factors that lead us to say, "Well yes, these things are signs of an impending recession, generally, but not always." Because we might be in one of these exceptional circumstances, although we do not think so, we have to qualify our claim. So, I have drawn an arrow up from these exceptions to the word "probably" which I have inserted before the claim. "Probably, the economy is entering into a recession." The word "probably" also reminds us that we are not dealing with matters that we can establish with certainty. We are not dealing with matters we can deduce, or with conclusions that follow absolutely. When we say, "The economy is probably entering a recession," we are saying we have enough reason to believe it, that we ought to take action based on it, whether it is individual consumers, or from the standpoint of public policy, as the case may be. So, this version of the diagram fills in the content of a specific argument, so we can see in the example we are working with what each of these parts of the argument really is.

With this example, I think we have illustrated how this model, this layout, captures the essential components of the argument that the economy is heading into a recession. Now, I should tell you that while we have covered a lot of ground in this lecture, we basically have a model of a very simple argument—only one claim at a time, and a limited range of evidence and warrants. What happens when arguments are more complex? Find out next time.

Lecture Six
Complex Structures of Argument

Scope:

The diagram presented in Lecture Five will help us to understand a simple argument structure, but most arguments are embedded in more complex structures. What is a claim in one part of the argument may be evidence in another, and subsidiary claims are joined together to support a main claim or resolution. This lecture will explore the basic ways—multiple, coordinative, and subordinative—that arguments are joined in more complex structures. Being able to map and analyze these structures offers considerable advantages, and these will be reviewed briefly. There are limitations to the use of argument diagrams and models, and these will be acknowledged briefly at the end of the lecture.

Outline

I. The model developed in the last lecture is of a simple argument.

    A. There is a single claim.

    B. The argument develops sequentially, as in conversation.

    C. In contrast, many arguments are complex, involving multiple claims, and must be developed without knowing exactly what the audience will accept and dispute.

II. In a complex argument, the resolution is a statement capturing the substance of the controversy.

    A. It is the ultimate claim on which judgment is sought.

    B. It may be explicitly stated or it may be implicit in the discourse of the participants.

    C. It should be capable of being captured in a single, declarative sentence.

    D. As with other claims, there are different types of resolutions—fact, definition, value, and policy—with different proof requirements.

III. Issues are implicit in the resolution.

    A. A precise definition of *issue* is important.

1. The term is used loosely in everyday language.
2. Issues are questions inherent in a controversy and vital to the success of the resolution.
B. Issues can be located in different ways.
    1. They can be located by examining the text of the resolution.
    2. They can be located by examining the underlying context.
    3. They can be derived from a pattern of claims and responses.
C. Potential issues minus uncontested issues equals actual issues.

IV. There are three major patterns for organizing complex arguments.
    A. Arguments may be arranged in a series (or subordinative) structure.
        1. Each argument is dependent on the others.
        2. All the arguments must be carried in order to carry the resolution.
    B. Arguments may be arranged in a convergent (or coordinative) structure.
        1. Each argument is independent of the others.
        2. The whole group of arguments, though, must be carried in order to carry the resolution.
    C. Arguments may be arranged in a parallel (or multiple) structure.
        1. Each argument is independent of the others.
        2. Each argument separately is sufficient to carry the resolution.

V. Colin Powell's 2003 speech to the United Nations Security Council illustrates the structure of complex arguments.
    A. The resolution was something like, "The Security Council should authorize the use of force in Iraq."
        1. This is a policy claim.
        2. It raises the standard *topoi* of a policy claim. (The concept of *topoi*, or "stock issues," is discussed in Lecture Seven.)

B. Several subsidiary arguments were used to support the resolution.

    1. The Iraqi regime is tyrannical.

    2. Iraq supports terrorists.

    3. Sanctions have been effective.

    4. Iraq has, or soon will have, weapons of mass destruction, making urgent action necessary.

C. The original structure of the argument was a combination of parallel and convergent.

D. After the fact, supporters of the President's policy treated the arguments as purely parallel, whereas opponents treated them as convergent.

VI. Although they are useful for pedagogical purposes, the use of argument models (like those developed in the last two lectures) has been criticized.

A. Models are instruments for identifying and analyzing arguments, not necessarily for constructing them.

B. Models "abstract out" subtle features of language, emphasis, and presentation that are integral to actual arguments.

C. Models suggest that a linearity of movement runs from the evidence to the claim, which is not characteristic of actual arguments.

D. Nevertheless, argument models are helpful if properly used.

    1. They help us to identify the components of an argument.

    2. They alert us to the internal dynamics of the argument.

    3. They permit a "translation" of different arguments into a common form to make comparisons easier.

Essential Reading:

Frans van Eemeren et al., *Argumentation: Analysis, Evaluation, Presentation*, pp. 63–78.

Charles Arthur Willard, "On the Utility of Descriptive Diagrams for the Analysis and Criticism of Arguments," in William L. Benoit, Dale Hample, and Pamela J. Benoit, eds., *Readings in Argumentation*, pp. 239–257.

Supplementary Reading:

Austin J. Freeley and David L. Steinberg, *Argumentation and Debate*, pp. 35–49.

Richard D. Rieke and Malcolm O. Sillars, *Argumentation and Critical Decision Making*, pp. 41–62.

J. W. Patterson and David Zarefsky, *Contemporary Debate: Critical Thinking for Reasoned Decision Making*, pp. 16–27.

Questions to Consider:

1. Under what circumstances might a series, parallel, or convergent structure each be the most productive and useful for an arguer?

2. How can the limitations of argument diagrams be minimized so that the diagrams will assist in the analysis and evaluation of arguments?

Relationships among Controversies, Resolutions, Issues, and Claims

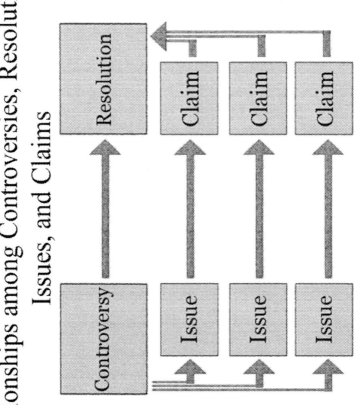

Series Structure of Argument

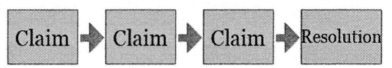

Parallel Structure of Argument

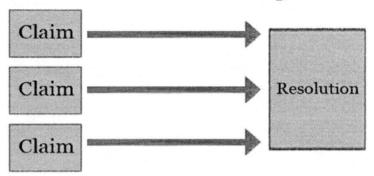

Convergent Structure of Argument

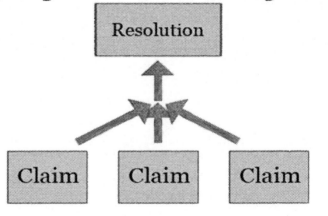

Diagram of Colin Powell's Speech to the United Nations

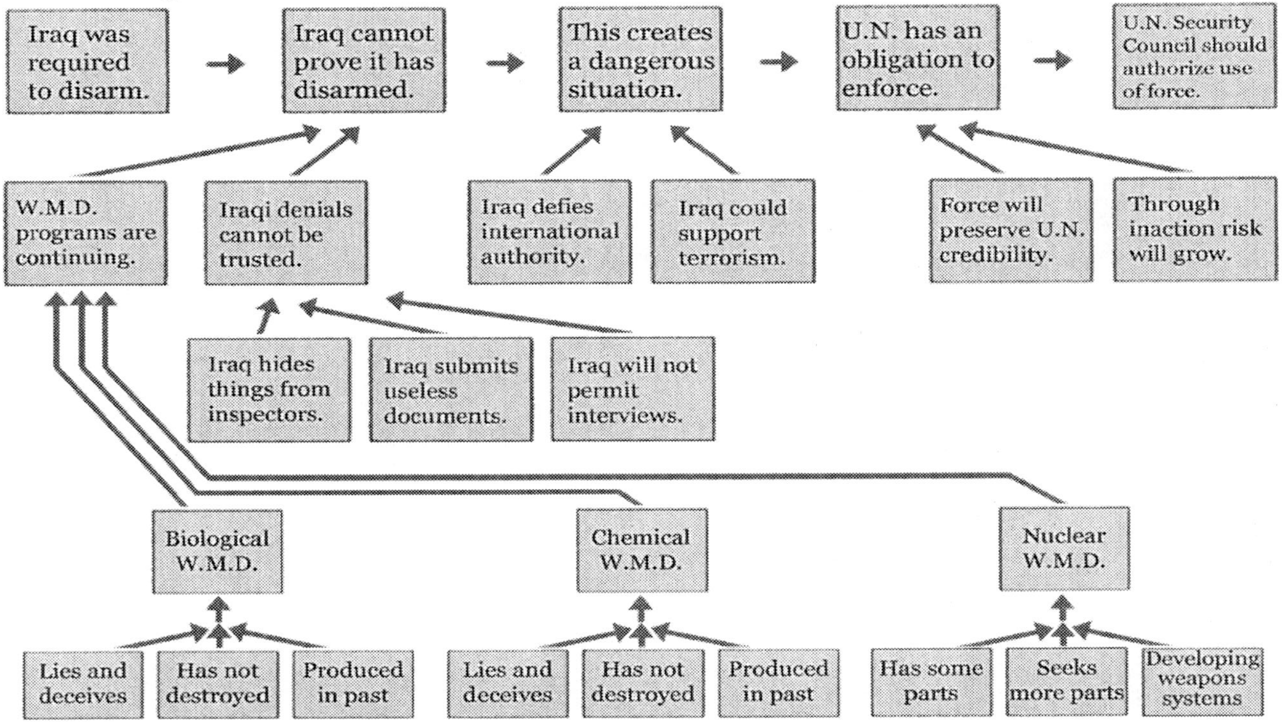

Lecture Six—Transcript
Complex Structures of Argument

It's good to be back with you again. As I warned at the end of the last lecture, the model that we had developed at that point was of a very simple argument. There was only single claim, and the argument was developing sequentially, as if in a conversation. Only one point was at issue at a time. Many arguments aren't like that. They're much more complex. There may be multiple claims, all at issue at one time, some of them supporting other claims; and the argument may have to be developed all at once without knowing exactly how an opponent or an audience would respond to it. This would happen in a formal speech, for example, or in a written essay, where there's not the back and forth interaction, and the speaker or writer has to anticipate all of the possible responses, and build them into the original argument. These are arguments that are more complex in nature, and that's the focus of this lecture.

In a complex argument there is one main claim—the one that captures the substance of the controversy—and we call it the resolution. Any controversy could be seen as posing a major question. When two friends get together and talk about interfaith marriages the underlying question in the controversy is, "Do interfaith marriages generally succeed?" When in a policy-making context, people talk about whether or not the United States should develop a national missile defense system, the underlying question that controversy is trying to address is something like, "How should the United States deal with the threats of terrorism?" If we imagine an answer to the question that poses the controversy, that answer is what we mean by the resolution. It's the position that one of the advocates in the controversy will defend. It's the ultimate claim on which judgment is being sought. It may be explicitly stated, or it made be implicit in the discourse of the participants. But it should be capable at least of being captured in a single declarative sentence; and, like any other kind of claim, there are four different types of resolutions: fact, definition, value, and policy.

Implicit in the controversy are certain issues that an advocate will need to defend in order to uphold the resolution. The subordinate claims that the advocate advances will be answers to those issues. Let me say a bit about issues. The word "issue" is used very loosely in ordinary discourse. Sometimes it's used to mean any disagreement, as when one person says to another, "Don't make an issue of it," meaning, "Let's not discuss it." We have a more precise meaning for the term issue.

Issues are the questions that are inherent in a controversy and vital to the success of the resolution. The key terms obviously are "inherent" and "vital." When I say that issues are inherent in a controversy, I mean they grow naturally from it. If we were to ask the question, "Do interfaith marriages succeed?" we would be led naturally to a series of other questions. What counts as an interfaith marriage? What do we mean by success? How will we know whether or not it succeeds? And so on. Those are inherent in the larger controversy. If we had a resolution, that interfaith marriages generally fail, in order to sustain that resolution, we have to be able to speak to and answer those issues. They're vital to it. If we can't answer the issue satisfactorily, then we can't sustain the resolution. Issues are inherent in the controversy, and they're vital to the success of the resolution.

At this point, let me take just a moment and put together the relationship among controversies, issues, resolutions, and claims. If you're following on video, you might want to look at this chart that I'm going to describe, where we can imagine one box that I have at the upper left labeled "controversy," and then an arrow pointing to another box at the upper right that's labeled "resolution." This tells that from the controversy we derive the resolution. The controversy poses the question; the resolution is an answer to the question that one of the advocates will seek to defend. Then, going down from the controversy, there is an area that leads to series of boxes, each of which I've labeled "issue." Each one of these boxes is a question that's inherent in the controversy. It grows out of the controversy and the answer to those questions—to the right of each of those issue boxes, you could draw an arrow to a box and label it "claim," and that would be a statement that would be made to answer the issue. The claims respond to the issues. The issues grow out of the controversy. Those claims, taken together, lead back up by an arrow pointing up on the right side of the chart to the resolution. The issues grow out of the controversy. They're answered with statements or claims that are vital to the success of the resolution. That, then, is the relationship among these four key terms: controversy, resolution, issue, and claim.

Of course, not every issue will be contested. Some may not be in dispute. The parties might agree to them. So we can say that potential issues minus the uncontested issues will yield the actual issues in the dispute.

Let's consider an example to see how the issues work. In February of 2003, then Secretary of State Colon Powell addressed the United Nations Security Council seeking approval for military action against Iraq. He was defending a policy resolution, which we might state as "the Security Council should authorize the use of force in Iraq." His speech was long—it was 16 pages long in print—but if we read it carefully, we'll see that he's addressing a controversy, "Does Iraq pose a threat to world peace?" The resolution answers the controversy, and we'll see that he examines the following four issues.

First, "Is there a problem?" His answer is "Yes," and the claim he advances is, "Iraq is developing weapons of mass destruction, which it might put into the hands of terrorists." A second issue he examines is "What is to blame?" His answer in the form of a claim: "Saddam Hussein has violated United Nations resolutions, and the UN has not enforced them." The third issue he takes up, although only briefly, is, "Will the proposal solve the problem?" He says "Yes, it will either destroy the weapons or remove the government." Finally number four: "On balance, will the proposal be better?" Secretary Powell's claim is, "Yes, because it will remove a threat to peace in the region, and it will bolster the credibility of the UN."

I should make clear that Secretary Powell does not label these issues in the way that I have just done, but if you read his speech and examine what he's saying, you will see that in that speech, he develops responses to these issues. The issues grow naturally out of the question of the controversy, "Does Iraq pose a threat to world peace." These are issues that he has to answer successfully in order to sustain the resolution that the United Nations should authorize the use of force. We'll consider later how Powell developed his arguments, and how well he defended them. But for now, notice how he applied the theory that we've been describing. The controversy gives rise to a series of questions; these are the issues to which Powell responds with claims that taken together support the resolution.

Let's consider how complex arguments like Secretary Powell's are organized. The organization of complex arguments is also complex, but there are three basic patterns. I'll describe each and show you a model of what each looks like. The models highlight the relationship between individual claims and the resolution. Of course, each box in these models containing a claim is also part of an argument for which there is evidence, and inference, and the warrant, as we discussed last time; but these diagrams would get far too complicated if we put in all of those elements again.

Let's just remember that each one of the boxes we're about to see could be blown up into the model that we discussed last time. What are the three basic patterns? First complex arguments can be arranged in a series structure, sometimes called by writers a subordinative structure. This is like a series circuit in physics, and that's where the analogy comes from; or like the old-fashioned Christmas tree lights, where if one of the light bulbs goes out the whole string of them goes out, because the current passes through each one successively. Each one depends upon all the others. That's a characteristic of the series structure of argument. Each claim leads to another in a chain, and each one depends upon all the others if the claim is going to be established.

For instance, let's suppose that the resolution that we want to defend is the claim, airline mistakes cost me my job. We ask how we're going to defend this resolution. Here are our subordinate claims: first, my luggage was mis-tagged when I went on a business trip; because it was mis-tagged, it was sent to the wrong city; because it was sent to the wrong city, I did not have valuable documents and papers that I had packed in my luggage; because I was missing those documents and papers, I gave a poor presentation in the city where I was being sent by my company; and because I gave a poor presentation, I was fired from my job. You see here how we have a classic series structure. Every step depends upon everything that's happened before it. If we could break one of the links in the chain, we'd break the whole chain of argument. Each claim leads to another; each depends upon the others; and all of the arguments must be carried in order to carry the resolution. You might think, therefore, that this is a poor way to organize arguments, but consider this: the series structure also creates a kind of momentum, where each one of the steps pushes you forward toward the next step, so that if you think you can carry the series, you get some extra force from the cumulative kind of momentum that the series structure generates. That's one way that we could organize a complex argument, in a series pattern.

A second pattern: we could organize our arguments in a convergent structure, sometimes called a coordinative structure. Here's the difference between convergent and series. Remember, in series we said that each argument depends upon the others. In a convergent structure, each argument is independent of the other arguments; each claim stands on its own. But like the series circuit, it's the totality of the arguments that converge to establish the resolution. That's why this structure is called convergent. The arguments don't depend on each other, but we need their cumulative weight to support the resolution.

Let's consider this resolution: airline travel is becoming more unpleasant. That's the main claim that we want to establish, and we've got a structure of subordinate claims that will establish it. For instance, we have one claim that says, flights are often delayed. Another one says, planes are really overcrowded. The third one says, the airlines don't serve food anymore. The fourth one says, airport security after September 11th is really intrusive. Another one says, airports have become tense places where you really can't relax anymore. Another one says, more passengers are rude these days. Another one says, people are always using their cell phones and you have to overhear their conversations. All of these things work together to support the claim that airline travel is becoming more unpleasant, the resolution that we're trying to defend. One of those supporting claims by itself might not be all that significant. We might dismiss any one of those things as a minor nuisance, not really a signal of unpleasantness. But if you put them all together: if you have delayed flights, and crowded planes, and no food, and tense airports—you have all of those things together—their convergence supports the resolution that airline travel is becoming more unpleasant.

A third pattern: arguments may be arranged in a parallel structure, sometimes called a multiple structure. Again, the analogy is to physics: a parallel circuit is one in which the current passes through, and if one light goes out the rest of them stay lit; each stands on its own. Each argument is independent of the others, just like in the convergent structure; but unlike the convergent structure, each one by itself is sufficient to carry the resolution. This time we might imagine a diagram where we've got a group of boxes, each representing an individual claim. We've got a resolution over here, and each one of the boxes independently has an arrow going from it to the resolution, because each one by itself would show that the resolutions are probably true.

Consider this example, still about our airlines. Here are our different claims: Airline prices don't make sense. Airline schedules are inconvenient. Connections are often missed. To obtain discount fares, you have to buy tickets way in advance before knowing the details of your plans. Websites and online reservations are confusing. Reservation agents don't respond well to questions. Those would all be claims supporting the resolution, airline travel is difficult to plan. In this example, each one of the claims by itself establishes that travel is difficult to plan. If prices don't make sense, it's hard to plan. If the schedules are inconvenient, it's hard to plan. If you can't make your connections, it's hard to plan. If you have to buy your ticket too early, it's hard to plan, and so on. Each one separately and independently helps to establish the resolution.

We have the three basic organizational plans for complex arguments: series, convergent, and parallel. Now, let's go back to Colin Powell's 2003 speech and see how he organized his arguments. I warn you, this is a complex argument, and so it has a complex structure. If you're on video you might follow this diagram. If you're in your car, please don't stop now to look at the outline; check it later. First, if you notice across the top of the chart, the main argument that Secretary Powell is making is developed in a series structure. The resolution that he's defending is at the upper right: "The Security Council should authorize the use of force in Iraq." How does he get there? Follow his argument, he says, "Iraq was required by the UN to disarm." Then, "Iraq cannot prove that it's done so." Then, "This creates a dangerous situation." And then, "The UN has an obligation to enforce its resolutions; therefore, the Security Council should authorize the use of force."

It's a series structure because each one of the steps depends upon the ones that have come before it. It wouldn't matter whether Iraq could prove that its weapons of mass destruction if the UN hadn't required it to do so. We wouldn't be in a dangerous situation if we weren't unsure about whether Iraq had given up its weapons. The Security Council wouldn't need to authorize the use of force if there weren't a UN obligation. There wouldn't be a UN obligation if the situation weren't dangerous. It's arranged in a series. If you thought before that a series is an inherently weak structure, think again because what this series does is it creates the sense of momentum for Secretary Powell's argument.

Now notice something interesting: as he develops each one of the steps in that chain, several of them are developed with a parallel structure. For instance, look at the second step up at the top: "Iraq cannot prove that it's disarmed its weapons of mass destruction." Secretary Powell gives you two separate arguments, independent of each other but both supporting that. First, that Iraq's weapons of mass destruction programs are continuing, and second, that Iraqi denials can't be trusted. Each one of those by itself is a reason to conclude that Iraq cannot prove that it has disarmed its weapons of mass destruction. Now, for added measure, each one of those two is independently supported by three arguments in another parallel structure. How do we know that the weapons of mass destruction programs are continuing? The Secretary argues, biological weapons are continuing; chemical weapons programs are continuing; nuclear weapons programs are continuing. Each one of those by itself separately would prove that Iraq is continuing its WMD programs. And, "Iraqi denials cannot be trusted," is supported by three separate independent arguments. Iraq hides things from the inspectors; Iraq submits useless documents to mislead the UN; and Iraq won't permit interviews of scientists outside the country. Each one separately and by itself is a reason to conclude that "Iraqi denials can't be trusted." This argument, that Iraq can't prove it has disarmed, is supported by parallel structures, which in turn are supported by other parallel structures.

Look across the top line at the next step. This creates a dangerous situation. Secretary Powell has another parallel structure, two separate reasons why it's a dangerous situation: because it flouts and defies the international authority of the UN, and because weapons of mass destruction could be given to terrorists. Each one of those is a reason for concluding the situation is dangerous: if the UN's authority is questioned, or if terrorists obtain weapons of mass destruction.

Look at the next step across the top: the UN has an obligation to enforce its resolutions—another parallel structure. It has an obligation, first of all, to preserve its own credibility, its own relevance, as Secretary Powell said. And second, it has an obligation because the risk will only grow; and if it doesn't act now, the threat to peace will be even more serious in the future, when terrorists may get access to the weapons of mass destruction.

Look what we've seen so far about Secretary Powell's argument. His main line argument is developed in series structure, but almost every one of the steps is, in turn, developed in a parallel structure.

Now notice one more thing: let's go back to the weapons of mass destruction programs— biological, chemical, and nuclear. Every one of those claims—that Iraq's developing biological weapons, chemical weapons, nuclear weapons—is supported by a convergent structure. Look at biological, for example. Secretary Powell says, "Iraq has been producing biological weapons in the past; it can't account for their destruction; and it lies about what its doing."

Those three arguments are independent of one another, but they work together. They converge to establish that Iraq is producing biological weapons. The fact that Iraq has done so in the past wouldn't be enough by itself. The fact that you can't prove that old weapons have been destroyed wouldn't be enough by itself. The fact that Iraq is deceiving the inspectors wouldn't be enough by itself. But put together, they converge to establish that Iraq is developing biological weapons. The very same arguments, the very same convergent structure, are used to show that Iraq is developing chemical weapons. With respect to nuclear weapons, there's again a convergent structure. Iraq has some parts already, is trying to get missing parts, and is developing the weapons system to deliver the weapons.

Notice what we see in Secretary Powell's speech. We see a complex argument that uses all of the organizational patterns, and combines them in ways to create a map of the argument that I've represented in this diagram. Again, I hasten to point out, Secretary Powell doesn't have a chart like this; he doesn't proceed in exactly this order; and he doesn't label his arguments. But we can; and when we do, we can understand what he's doing in this argument, and how it gets put together.

Of course, what we've done with Secretary Powell's speech, you could do with any newspaper editorial, op-ed column, or any other example of an argument. We identified the resolution; we figured out the issues; we diagramed the structure of the argument; and then, if we wanted to, we could go back to the last lecture, and within individual arguments, we could show the evidence, and the influence, and the warrant, as well as the claim.

Why should we do that? Why should you practice the kind of argument diagramming? It enables you to understand what's going on in the argument. Most of us who didn't read Secretary Powell's speech, and didn't diagram it out, have only a sound byte or two to go on to figure out what he really said. We could actually diagram it and structure the argument out. Also, understanding what Secretary Powell did is the first step to enable us to appraise the quality of his argument. Secretary Powell's speech has been criticized in the aftermath of the failure to find weapons of mass destruction. Did Secretary Powell make a mistake because, in fact, the weapons didn't turn up? Was his argument poor? Or was his argument good and reasonable, even though the weapons didn't turn up? To answer that question, we have to be able to know what he argued and how he went about it, and that's what we gain by diagramming the argument.

We also are able to start thinking about alternatives. What if Secretary Powell had not separated out biological, chemical, and nuclear weapons? What if he had not used a parallel structure for why the UN has an obligation to enforce its resolutions? What if he had not grounded the main line of his argument in a series structure? We could go on and on and on with each one of the steps of the argument. We could imagine alternatives, other ways to do it; and then, for practice, we could figure out what each of us might do if confronted with the particular situation of the argument that we're examining. I know that few of us are ever going to have the opportunity to address the UN Security Council; but if you do this with a letter to the editor, or an editorial in the local newspaper, or in a conversation that you have in your family, the same process works just as well, and we can get some real insight into the nature of the arguments. In other words, I'm suggesting that being able to model and diagram complex as well as simple arguments is highly useful for pedagogical purposes, as a way to teach ourselves about argument.

You should know that there are some theorists who object to this whole process of diagramming arguments. They say that it gives the arguments a mistaken linear quality, that there's really not this clear progression; and indeed, if you go back and read Powell's speech, he doesn't progress clearly in the way that I've described. They say it's misleading to try and diagram the argument this way. They say that diagramming is an analytical exercise only and it shouldn't be confused with actually building the arguments. Well and good. We can accept that there are limitations to the diagrams, but there's a great value that they serve; and I think we've seen how the serve the value in the example that we have described. In addition to enabling us to analyze arguments, these tools are also useful when we build our own arguments; and we'll take up that topic next time.

Lecture Seven
Case Construction—Requirements and Options

Scope:

The complex structure of argument discussed in Lecture Six can be regarded as a case, the pattern of arguments used to support a claim. In assembling a case, arguers must be sure to address all the issues raised by the claim in the particular situation. An aid to identifying the issues is the concept of *topoi*, meaning "places," which are patterns of issues that recur with given types of claims and situations. Addressing the issues will satisfy an initial burden of proof. In meeting these requirements, arguers have choices about what arguments to use and how to arrange them. In individual arguments, choices are made about which evidence to use and how to arrange it. This lecture will identify the key choices and the factors that go into making them.

Outline

I.   A case is the structure of subsidiary claims and evidence selected for supporting or opposing a resolution for a specific audience.

    A. Constructing a case involves choices from a broader range of arguments that are potentially available.

        1. Choices are made regarding which arguments to use.

        2. Within arguments, choices are made regarding which evidence to use.

        3. Choices are made regarding how to arrange arguments and, within arguments, how to arrange evidence.

    B. Choices are audience-specific.

        1. They adapt to a particular audience the arguments that were formed with a broader audience in mind.

        2. They combine creativity with constraint.

    C. The principal constraint on case construction, as noted in the last lecture, is the need to address all the issues in the resolution.

II. *Topoi* ("stock issues") offer a shortcut to locating issues in a given case.

    A. *Topoi* (literally "places") are issues always raised when addressing resolutions of a given type.

        1. They are recurrent patterns of analysis.

        2. As noted above, by classifying the resolution into a certain type, we can determine the *topoi* for it.

    B. For resolutions of fact, the *topoi* can be identified.

        1. What is the criterion for assessing truth?

        2. Has the criterion been satisfied?

    C. For resolutions of definition, the *topoi* can be identified.

        1. Is the interpretation relevant?

        2. Is it fair?

        3. How should we choose among competing interpretations?

    D. For resolutions of value, the *topoi* can be identified.

        1. Is the value truly as good or bad as alleged?

        2. Which among competing values should be preferred?

        3. Has the value been properly applied to the specific situation?

    E. For resolutions of policy, the *topoi* can be identified.

        1. Is there a problem?

        2. Where is credit or blame due?

        3. Will the proposal solve the problem?

        4. On balance, will the proposal be better?

III. Addressing the issues will meet the advocate's initial burden of proof.

    A. The supporter of the resolution must present a case for it that would be compelling in the absence of any response.

    B. This burden is met by satisfactorily answering the issues raised by the resolution.

    C. Once this burden is met, the burden of rejoinder comes into play.

        1. This is the responsibility to keep the discussion going, analogous to the production burden in law.

        2. This burden shifts back and forth between the arguers.

3. Its being met by a supporter of the resolution means that an opponent must now respond.
4. The burden of rejoinder prevents the argument from stopping.
5. It also prevents arguers from just repeating their previous positions without extending them to answer subsequent challenges.

IV. Regarding the selection of arguments for the case, the key considerations are whether the arguments are strong enough and how many to include.

   A. Strength is a function of two main factors.

      1. It is a function of the listener's prior adherence to the evidence or the likelihood that adherence can be obtained.

      2. It is a function of the relevance of the claim to the resolution.

      3. Each of these factors is affected by other variables, such as the degree of probability, the time frame of the argument, and the argument's consistency with common sense and generally accepted values.

   B. Arguments in the debate about Social Security reform illustrate the concept of strength.

      1. The argument that the Social Security trust fund eventually may be depleted is relatively strong.

      2. The argument that African Americans are hurt by Social Security because they have lower life expectancy than whites is relatively weak.

   C. Determining the amplitude (number and range of arguments) is affected by more factors than just the amount of time available.

      1. Amplitude can be increased to offset the inconclusiveness of individual arguments or to hedge against the heterogeneity of the audience.

      2. Increasing amplitude has risks, however: A poor argument reflects badly on all choices and on the arguer's credibility, and piling up arguments may seem overly defensive.

      3. With appropriate care in framing arguments, some of the dangers of increasing amplitude can be minimized.

D. Similar considerations affect the selection of evidence in individual arguments.

V. Choices are also made regarding the organization of individual arguments.

    A. Once the overall organizational structure is determined, within a parallel or convergent structure, there are additional choices to be made.

        1. One choice is whether to put the strongest arguments first or last.

        2. One choice is whether to anticipate and answer objections before they are made.

        3. One choice is whether to proceed from the familiar to the unfamiliar.

        4. These choices are matters of logical indifference but rhetorical significance.

    B. Independent arguments follow several common organizational patterns.

        1. They can be arranged in chronological order.

        2. They can be arranged in spatial order.

        3. They can be arranged in categories.

        4. They can use a cause-effect or a problem-solution structure.

        5. They can be arranged as comparisons or contrasts.

        6. They can rely on the method of residues.

    C. It is not necessary to organize by reference to the list of *topoi,* so long as each of the *topoi* is addressed effectively.

VI. The assembling of the case in Lyndon B. Johnson's 1965 voting rights message offers an instructive example.

    A. Johnson spoke to the relevant *topoi.*

    B. Johnson arranged his arguments in a complex structure, giving priority to matters of principle.

    C. Johnson made careful strategic choices about the ordering of his arguments.

Essential Reading:

Austin J. Freeley and David L. Steinberg, *Argumentation and Debate: Critical Thinking for Reasoned Decision Making*, chapter 12.

Chaim Perelman, *The Realm of Rhetoric*, pp. 138–152.

Supplementary Reading:

Richard D. Rieke and Malcolm O. Sillars, *Argumentation and Critical Decision Making*, pp. 225–247.

J. W. Patterson and David Zarefsky, *Contemporary Debate*, pp. 59–69.

Questions to Consider:

1. In what ways do the choices discussed in this lecture reflect both creativity and constraint? How can creativity be enhanced in the face of constraint?

2. How does an arguer know when the case is strong enough to satisfy the initial burden of proof and trigger the burden of rejoinder?

Lecture Seven—Transcript
Case Construction—Requirements and Options

Welcome back. We talked last time about the structure of complex arguments, in which several claims are organized so that they support or oppose a main claim called the resolution. There is a word for this set of arguments, and that word is a case, the subject of this lecture. The particular set of arguments that we put together to support a resolution or to oppose a resolution for a particular audience is what we mean by the term case. In order to introduce this concept, I'd like to remind us of a diagram that we talked about last time, when we talked about the relationship among controversies, resolutions, issues, and claims. You may recall that I said that a controversy gives rise to a resolution. Underlying that controversy—inherent in it and vital to the success of the resolution—are a series of issues: questions that are answered by claims; and the claims together support the resolution.

If you look again at the right-hand part of that diagram, in which the claims come together to support the resolution, that's what the case consists of: the grouping or the arrangement of those claims. Taken together the claims must speak to the issues. They must answer all of the issues that are salient in the given controversy; otherwise the case won't be plausible on its face. The technical term for that, by the way, is prima facie, which means "on first face." If you don't have a case that really speaks to the issues, then just upon hearing it, it won't seem plausible; it won't seem like it answers the question.

Having said that, I have to tell you this diagram we looked at before is a bit oversimplified. Not all of the issues will come up in an actual controversy. Some will be stipulated; some issues will be combined; one claim may speak to multiple issues; and sometimes there'll be multiple claims speaking to a single issue. I want us to focus more on how these claims get put together, and what the relationship is between the claims and the resolution. To do that I'd like to talk about how we build a case.

There's always a broader range of material available than can be used. We could imagine more possible claims than we could put together to support any given resolution in any amount of time, and so we make choices. We make two kinds of choices: we make choices of selection and choices of arrangement. The selection choices tell us what we'll pick out from among the range of possibilities, and the arrangement choices tell us how we'll put them together and what sort of structure we will use. By the way, we make these choices not only with respect to arguments that make up the case, but also with respect to evidence within individual arguments. Just as there are more claims than we could ever use to support a resolution, so there is more potential evidence than we could ever use to support a given claim.

What governs these choices then? Here's where the audience comes into play. Remember, we've said all along that one characteristic of ordinary argumentation, as opposed to formal logic, is that it's presented in a context. There's an audience, and one of the factors that governs the choices we make is the audience. We want to pick from those arguments that are available, the ones that will be particularly important or meaningful to the given audience that we happen to address. These choices really combine creativity and constraint. We're thinking creatively when we try to imagine all of the possibilities and see what our range of options is, and we're constrained by the fact of the audience—by the audience composition, the audience predispositions, the audience beliefs or values that we want to appeal to as we put this structure of arguments together. Of course, a very important constraint is that the case speaks to all the issues, so that it will be prima facie.

Let's start with that. How do we find the issues? Given a resolution, how do we really know what the issues are? There are several different ways that we could discover the issues. For one, we could ask questions about the text of the resolution: take each one of the key terms in the resolution and see what kinds of questions it poses. This is what I did in the example of interfaith marriage when I said, "What do we mean by succeed? How do we know if interfaith marriages succeed," and so on?

A second way we can find the issues is by looking at the underlying context of the resolution. What's going on out in the world that this controversy is dealing with? If we applied that method to the resolution that the United States should develop a national missile defense system, we might find issues like the following: Was the Bush Administration wise to abrogate the Antiballistic Missile Treaty? Will a national missile defense system work? Is the technology available for national missile defense? Do the costs exceed the benefits? And so on. Notice that, unlike the interfaith marriage example, these questions don't come from the wording or the text of the resolution itself. They instead come from the context. They require us to know about what's going on out in the world that the resolution is dealing with; so that's a second way we can do it.

A third way we would could do it would be to gather up a good sample of what people have said about the resolution, and then figure out, of all that sample, what they agree upon, which we can then set aside. This is not in dispute. It can be stipulated. Then, when you see what's left, when you see what they disagree about, you can say, "Well, these are the central points of disagreement."

All of these methods are perfectly good. Each of them will lead us to discover the issues that are inherent in the controversy; but they have one problem: they can be cumbersome. They can be really time-consuming. Fortunately, there's a shortcut that what we can use to discover the issues, and the shortcut works so well that it's probably the method that's used most often of all. This shortcut reflects the fact that certain types of issues recur with resolutions of a given type. Once we know what kind of resolution we have—fact, definition, value, or policy—we will know what categories of issues to look for. These categories are called *topoi,* a Greek word that means "place." They are places in the mind, metaphorical places that one goes to look to find issues.

So what are the *topoi*? They were identified pretty well by the ancient Greeks and Romans. For a resolution of fact, they are fairly simple. 1) How will we know if the statement is true? That is, what are our criteria? 2) Are the criteria satisfied?

For a resolution of definition such as, that the fetus is a person, the *topoi* would be as follows: 1) Is the interpretation relevant? 2) Is the interpretation fair? 3) How do we choose among competing interpretations?

For a resolution of value: 1) Is the condition truly good or bad, as alleged? 2) Has the value been properly applied to the situation at hand? 3) How do we choose among competing values?

Finally, for resolutions of policy: 1) Is there a problem? 2) Where is the credit or blame for the problem due? 3) Will the proposal solve the problem? Will it work? 4) On balance, will things be better off with the proposal?

By the way, if your memory is good, you will notice that those four *topoi* are exactly the ones that I used in the last lecture to identify the issues that Secretary Powell addressed in his speech to the UN Security Council. The shortcut of finding *topoi* will tell us what sorts of issues come up with what kind of resolution or claim.

As we build our case, we want to be sure that we include something that speaks to each issue; doing that will make our case prima facie. We'll meet our initial burden of proof, and that will require that our opponent respond to what we've said. That requirement is the burden of rejoinder, and it will shift back and forth between us and our opponent as each responds to the other.

We want to be sure that the case meets our burden, but now we get to make choices about how to do it. Remember, I said that there are choices of selection and choices of arrangement. Let's take selection first. Here we want to further divide because there are two main kinds of selection choices: 1) Whether the arguments are strong enough; 2) How many arguments to include. We select according to strength and according to number.

Let's look at strength. How do we decide the strength of an argument? Here again, remember, in formal logic, arguments are either valid or invalid. The question of degrees of strength isn't an issue. In a probabilistic kind of situation, the sort we argue about everyday, strength is very much important. Strength is a function, first of all, of the listeners' prior adherence to the evidence in the argument. Remember, we said that disagreement is based in agreement. The evidence has to be agreed to as to its truth or the argument is not going to work very well. For instance, facts, or common knowledge, things that are widely shared, or things that could be easily established because of audience predispositions—all of these will work well as evidence, and arguments that contain them are likely to be strong. Secretary Powell used a lot of photographs and objects in his speech as evidence, out of a belief that pictures and objects don't lie. They're not subject to interpretation.

The other thing that governs the strength of an argument, besides whether the audience will accept its evidence, is how relevant the argument is to the resolution; that is to say, what happens to the resolution if the argument succeeds? Or what happens to the resolution if the argument fails. We could imagine at one extreme, the killer argument—the argument that just clinches the resolution.

For example, if we're talking about whether annual testing should be performed in elementary and secondary schools, if we could establish that annual testing disrupts the order of the curriculum, we would have a pretty powerful argument against doing it; because it would establish pretty strongly that there's a good reason not to, that something that's more fundamental will be imperiled if we do.

At the other extreme, we have arguments that fail to meet what I call the "so what" test. Even if you establish the argument is sound, so what? What difference does it make to the resolution? For example, whether the PSAT, the Preliminary Scholastic Assessment Test, is given in the 11th grade or in the 10th grade probably doesn't matter very much to the question of whether there should be annual testing. Yes, we can disagree about when is the best place to give that test, but it doesn't make much difference to the resolution that's at hand. Thus, a listener's prior adherence and the relevance of the claim to the resolution are factors that govern the strength of the claim.

Each of these, in turn, is affected by a number of other considerations. For instance, to what degree is the evidence speculative rather than certain? Audiences tend to prefer more certain to less certain evidence. To what degree does the claim rely on short-term urgent matters that are immediately before us? To what degree does it involve more distant, long-term considerations? People get more interested in things that are immediate and urgent. To what degree is the claim consistent with common sense, with what we already believe? You may remember in the 1980s, the government at one point claimed that catsup was a vegetable for the purpose of composition of school lunches. Most people are not inclined to believe that catsup is a vegetable, even if it could be shown that it is; and so an argument based on the assumption that catsup is a vegetable is not likely to be very strong as an argument. All of these elements affect whether listeners are predisposed to believe an argument, and how much good an argument does in establishing the resolution; these are strength considerations, the first of the choices that we make.

Arguments in the 2005 debate about Social Security reform illustrate the concept of strength. For example, one of the arguments advanced is that the Social Security trust fund eventually may be depleted. This is a relatively strong argument, even though it is long term rather than immediate; first of all, because it makes a big difference to the argument about Social Security reform if you don't have a trust fund there; and second, audiences pretty easily can accept that if you take out more than you put it in, eventually, the fund will go down.

In contrast, another argument that was advanced was that African Americans should favor private accounts because they have a lower life expectancy and, thereby, would get a greater benefit from it. This, I think most people would say is a relatively weak argument; first of all, because it offends our sense of justice—we ought to be trying to improve the life expectancy of African Americans, not conceding that it's going to be lower; and second, because it doesn't advance the resolution very much. It says that, here's a proposal that's popular with one segment of the population, not that it's a proposal that is good or that ought to be adopted. So, if we are choosing from arguments to defend President Bush's Social Security proposal, it would make more sense for us to pick the stronger argument, which is the first of the two that I described. That's strength.

The second selection question beyond strength is, how many arguments? What number and range of arguments to present? Why would we want to present more arguments? There are two reasons. First, because the arguments are inconclusive; they're not certain. We hedge our bets by presenting multiple arguments. We don't state the resolution on one single argument or on a very small number of arguments, because each one of them is inconclusive; so we hedge our bet by presenting more. Second, because an audience is likely to be heterogeneous, it will be made up of different kinds of people: some arguments will appeal to some people, and others will appeal to other people. And so we put arguments together for that reason and present more of them.

There is a technical term for this: it's called amplitude. Just like amplitude in physics is extending the width of a wave. Amplitude in argument is extending the range, widening the range of the argument by presenting more arguments in support of the resolution. However, presenting more arguments—increasing amplitude—also has risks. What are those?

For an example of a poor argument, let's say one of the ones in our range is a relatively weak argument; it reflects badly not only on itself, but on all of the other choices as well, and on they credibility of the arguer. Somebody tells you catsup is a vegetable. You will not only be unlikely to accept that catsup is a vegetable, but you'll begin wondering about some of the other claims that this person has made, and about what kind of a person would make such a claim as that catsup is a vegetable.

What's more, if we pile argument on argument on argument, it may sound like we don't have enough confidence in any of them. We may come off seeming defensive or even whiny. As we increase amplitude—as we present more arguments—we also increase the risk that we're going to present two arguments that are inconsistent with each other. One of the things we know about inconsistency in argument is that, while an inconsistency means only that both arguments can't be true—not that they're both false, but both can't be true—in fact, psychologically, audiences will often dismiss both.

Thus, when we increase the number of arguments we present, we run the risk that multiple arguments will be ignored or rejected by a given audience. There are dangers to presenting lots of arguments just as there are benefits to increasing the number of arguments. There's no recipe or formula that will tell us how many arguments to present. We have to figure out how many to use based on the circumstances of each specific situation, and understanding what the benefits and the risks are. In sum, we have factors of strength and factors of number that will govern our selection of arguments; within each argument, the same factors will govern our selection of evidence.

Now let's talk about the choices regarding arrangement. The first one we talked about last time: whether to use a series, or convergent, or parallel structure. We make that choice based on the subject matter we're discussing: what we think are the relationships among our claims, and what will be the easiest and most effective way to present those claims to an audience.

By the way, there's nothing that prevents us from combining these structures, just as we saw that Colin Powell did. Sometimes one will be stronger, sometimes another. There is, in principal, no reason that one of them is stronger or weaker than another. If we decide that the series structure is the one we want then, there's not a whole lot else about arrangement that we need to decide. We choose only whether start at the beginning of the chain and go forward—each claim leading to the next, to the next, to the next, to the resolution—or whether we start with the resolution and go backwards, and say the resolution is true because of this, and this is true because of this, and this because of this, and so on, back to the beginning of the chain. That's really all we have to decide.

But, with a convergent structure or a parallel structure, there are additional choices to be made. For instance, because it doesn't make any logical difference in a convergent or parallel structure which argument comes first, second, third, or fourth, we take the one that we think is the strongest. Where do we put it? Well, here the research is somewhat inconclusive. There's some research that says, put it first because it will capture the attention of the audience, and it will color their perceptions of all the rest of the arguments—a kind of halo effect. Other research says, put it last so that you leave the audience with a very strong impression with the strongest argument you could make. The first of these is called the primacy effect, and the second is called the recency effect. Some of the research favors one, some favors the other. The thing that they're consistent on is not to put the strongest argument in the middle; put it either at the beginning or at the end. We saw that Secretary Powell had a parallel structure in which he talked about biological, chemical, and nuclear weapons. He could have discussed the three in any order. You notice he put biological weapons first. He put nuclear weapons last. These are probably the two that pose the greatest threat worldwide.

There's another kind of choice to make: should you, up front, anticipate objections, and answer them, and build the answers into your structure? Here, the research suggests, if the audience is composed of people who are pretty well educated, or if the audience is known to be opposed to what you're arguing, in either of those cases, then it makes sense to build in, anticipate, and answer objections. Why? Because a highly educated audience will be thinking along, and exercising critical judgment, and they'll come up with objections anyway. So, it's important that you acknowledge them. Obviously, an audience that's opposed to you will have objections already in mind.

Another choice: should you proceed from what's most familiar to what's least familiar? This would be a kind of analogical structure. You start with what people know, and you make links from what they know to what they don't. That's been found to make understanding of unfamiliar material easier for an audience. On the other hand, it may sometimes be at odds with the logical connections among the parts of the argument. These choices—strongest first, strongest last, familiar to unfamiliar, whether to include and respond to objections—in a way, are all things that are matters of logical indifference. If you have a parallel structure or a convergent structure, each argument is going to work independently, no matter what order you put them in. These are questions that are rhetorically very significant. They decide how much salience an argument will have for listeners. They increase or reduce the ease with which listeners can process the argument, so that it's understood, and so, that it's more likely to succeed.

With arguments that are logically independent—that is a convergent or parallel structure— there are several very common organizational patterns that people often use. Because they are patterns, it is easy for a listener to follow along and anticipate what's coming next. One pattern is chronological—from past to present to future, or from future to present to past. One is spatial or geographical—from near to far; or from east to west, or north to south. One is to place items into familiar categories—the economic, the social, and the political. One pattern goes from cause to effect, or effect to cause; or problem to solution, or solution to problem. One is to compare and contrast. The one that we pick from among all these patterns will help listeners to follow along the structure of the argument. Notice, by the way, that in making these choices about selection and arrangement, it isn't necessary to organize the argument by reference to the list of the *topoi*; that is, in a policy resolution, we don't have to talk about the problem first, and then the blame, and then the cure, and so on. It only matters that we be sure to address each of the *topoi* effectively.

We've talked, here, about a number of constraints and choices. Let's look at how these work themselves out in a specific historical example. Of course, you could take Secretary Powell's speech that we discussed last time, and see how they worked out there; but I want to introduce another example: President Lyndon Johnson's defense of the Voting Rights Act in his speech of March of 1965.

President Johnson is not usually remembered as a really distinguished orator, but this speech was identified by a group of critics as one of the top 10 American speeches of the 20th century. It was delivered a week after the violence in Selma, Alabama, and it's remembered particularly for its emotion, in which a southern president addressed a joint session of Congress and uttered the words, "We shall overcome." It's also a speech that has a fairly rich argument to it. You can download the speech from the web—it's available at www.presidentialrhetoric.com—and you can see some of the choices that the president made.

First of all, he speaks to the relevant *topoi*. It's a problem-oriented, policy-oriented speech, and so he starts with the problem, that is, the denial of voting rights and violence against protesters. He blames the absence of any federal law to do anything about this as the cause. He suggests a new law to enforce constitutional rights that should be passed without delay, and he says that this will benefit the whole nation, not just African Americans, and that the right to vote secures all other rights.

If we look across his speech, we'll see that he does what he needs to do to meet the constraint of speaking to all of the issues. Notice how he selects his arguments. He picks arguments that the broad national audience will be likely to accept. For instance, he emphasizes that the right to vote is protected by the Constitution. It's a constitutional imperative. You may not like African Americans voting if you're a white Southern conservative, but you respect the Constitution, you honor the Constitution. Thus, the argument that it's a constitutional right is a strong argument; as is a moral appeal; as is an appeal to a sense of justice. Moreover, the president softens the blow to the South by paying homage to that region and talking about how important it is to the country.

You notice certain arrangement choices in that speech. The president discusses voting rights in an order so that the significance of the issue enlarges as he goes. He says it's a turning point in history; it's a basic fundamental issue; it transcends region or party; it's grounded in founding documents. He catalogs the depravations of voting rights. He then enlarges those from the specific bill to civil rights and the great society more generally. He proceeds from agreement to disagreement. This speech illustrates the choices of selection and arrangement. Now, we'll assume that the case has been put together, and next time we'll start considering how to respond to it.

Lecture Eight
Stasis—The Heart of the Controversy

Scope:

Stasis refers to the focal point of dispute, the point at which contending positions meet. It is determined by the choices that advocates make about what to stipulate and what to contest. So the first decision to be made in responding to a case is what the point of *stasis* will be. This lecture will explain and illustrate the concept, which is drawn from ancient theories of rhetoric. It will identify the four classical *stases*—conjecture, definition, quality, and place—and will illustrate each with examples of controversies. The concept, originally developed for legal disputes, will be treated more broadly and rendered applicable to policy controversies as well. Finally, employing the concept of *stasis* will be shown to be useful for both the arguer and the analyst of argument.

Outline

I. *Stasis* defines the focal point of a dispute.

    A. The term means "a point of rest" between opposing forces.

        1. Movement toward a goal cannot resume until the opposition is transcended.

        2. *Stasis* enables us to identify precisely what is in dispute and invites advocates to respond to it.

    B. The concept originated in classical rhetoric and originally was designed for courts of law.

II. Classical theory established four categories of *stasis*, each of which will be illustrated.

    A. *Stasis* in conjecture concerns whether an act occurred.

    B. *Stasis* in definition concerns what the act should be called.

    C. *Stasis* in quality concerns whether the act is justified.

    D. *Stasis* in place concerns whether the discussion is occurring in the proper forum.

III. Several features of the *stasis* categories deserve mention.

    A. What determines the *stasis* is not the original assertion but the response to it.

1. One may respond to a claim in a variety of ways.
2. The specific response, together with the original claim, will identify just what is at issue and, hence, where the *stasis* lies.
3. Therefore, an important preliminary to attacking a case is to determine where the *stasis* most usefully can be drawn.

B. Generally speaking, *stasis* is progressive.
   1. *Stasis* in definition implicitly concedes conjecture.
   2. *Stasis* in quality implicitly concedes conjecture and definition.
   3. Hence, an advocate should select a *stasis* as close to the beginning of the chain as can be sustained.
   4. Presenting multiple *stases* is better than shifting from one to another during the course of the argument.

C. As an exception to the above principle, *stasis* in place is pre-emptive.

IV. The concept of *stasis* can be adapted to nonlegal arguments.

   A. Multiple issues are in play, each with its own *stasis.*

   B. One popular model applies conjecture, definition, and quality to each of the four *topoi* for a resolution of policy.
   1. The *topoi* can be identified as *ill, blame, cure,* and *cost.*
   2. The result is a four-by-three matrix with 12 possible *stases* (ill-conjecture, ill-definition, and so on).

   D. *Stasis* in place usually is not applicable.

V. Failing to agree upon the *stasis* can have serious consequences for the argument.

   A. It can "hijack" the argument and change understanding of what it is, as the argument for Social Security reform demonstrates.

   B. It can result in the loss of the argument, as one writer suggests occurred in the famous Scopes trial.

   C. It can result in stalemate, as has occurred in the controversy about abortion rights.

VI. The concept of *stasis* has multiple uses.

- **A.** For the analyst, it enables one to locate the center of the dispute.
- **B.** For the arguer, it permits strategic choices about alternative means to respond to a given situation, as a preliminary to attack and defense.
- **C.** It also helps arguers to avoid the tendency to "talk past each other."

Essential Reading:

"*Stasis*," in Thomas O. Sloane, ed., *Encyclopedia of Rhetoric*, pp. 741–745.

Edward P. J. Corbett and Rosa A. Eberly, *The Elements of Reasoning*, 2nd ed., pp. 26–120.

Supplementary Reading:

Antonie Braet, "The Classical Doctrine of *Stasis* and the Rhetorical Theory of Argumentation," *Philosophy and Rhetoric* 20 (1987), pp. 79–93.

Ray Nadeau, "Hermogenes' *On Stases:* A Translation with an Introduction and Notes," *Communication Monographs* 31 (November 1964), pp. 361–424.

Questions to Consider:

1. Why is *stasis* more complex when applied to policy disputes than to legal controversies?

2. If the participants in a dispute have different opinions about where *stasis* lies, how can the dispute proceed?

Four by Three Matrix of Possible *Stasis* Points

	Conjecture	Definition	Quality
Ill	Do HMOs leave patients unsatisfied?	Is dissatisfaction a violation of rights?	Is the violation great enough to warrant change?
Blame	Do HMOs make the key decisions?	Is their discretion abused?	Should we consider other circumstances?
Cure	Can a bill of rights be devised?	Will it work?	How much abuse will it address?
Cost	What will a bill of rights cost patients?	Are they comparatively real costs?	Are the costs worth it?

Lecture Eight—Transcript
Stasis—The Heart of the Controversy

Hello again. Last time, we explored a series of concepts that explained what a case is and how one is put together. Now, we're about to explore how an advocate can respond to an opposing case. The very first thing we need to know is how to determine exactly what is in dispute. This is extremely important in order to focus the response on the true heart of the controversy and not to be misdirected.

For this purpose, I have to introduce a new term, really the only term that we're going to focus on in this lecture; that is the concept of *stasis*. *Stasis* is a Greek term sometimes the pronunciation has been Anglicized as *stasis*. It means literally "a point of rest or equilibrium." It is a nifty concept for figuring out exactly what's in dispute. We can think of it as a point between opposing forces. If you imagine a simple diagram in which you have an arrow moving in one direction and an arrow moving in the other direction to counteract it, there'll be this point—this almost metaphysical point— in between the two forces, where there's rest, where neither force can proceed because the other force opposes it.

If I can mix my metaphors, we can think of that point of rest as a fulcrum point because that's the point that the dispute turns on. Movement can't resume until that point is somehow overcome. The movement toward a goal, in other words, has got to get past this point of rest in order to proceed. What this fulcrum point tells us is precisely what's in dispute, what it is that's blocking the movement of these two forces. Once we know precisely what's in dispute, then the advocates are invited to respond to that focal point.

This concept of *stasis* originated in classical rhetoric. It was the anonymously written *Rhetorica ad Herennium*—in case you're interested—in which it first appeared. Cicero did a good job to refine and systematize it, as he did with many other concepts, and it was originally designed for advocacy in courts of law; although, as I think we'll see, it has a much broader application.

Let's unpack this concept. Let's figure out what it's all about. To do so, I want to consider a very simple example. Forget for the moment that we're among friends, and suppose I come up to you and I make the statement, "You stole my car." What are you going to do in response? We could imagine a whole variety of things you might do, but since we're discussing argumentation, let's assume you won't punch me in the nose. But you could make some different responses. Suppose you say, "No, I never had your car. I was never in possession of it all." Now, my assertion and your response establish a focal point for this disagreement. Did you have possession of my car? Did the act take place? This is referred to in the literature as *stasis* of conjecture: the question is, is it? Did it happen?

Suppose, on the other hand, I say, "You stole my car." And you reply, "No, I only borrowed it." Notice how this example is different from the first example. I've made the same assertion, "You stole my car." Your response: "No, I only borrowed it." Together, assertion and response established the fulcrum point, but the fulcrum point is not about whether the act occurred; it's about what we should call it, or how we should characterize it. This is referred to as *stasis* of definition: what is it? We have so far a *stasis* of conjecture and a *stasis* of definition.

Now, suppose I say, "You stole my car." Your response is, "Yes, but it's a good thing I did because I used it to take to the hospital someone who had fallen on your sidewalk when you hadn't shoveled the snow and ice off, and you would have been liable if I hadn't." Again, we have an assertion and a response. We have these two opposed argumentative forces. But now the dispute is over whether the act was justified—not whether it occurred, not what it should be called, but whether it was justified. It was justified, so you said, by extenuating circumstances. There was some special need that made it okay for you to do this. After all, you were not only protecting human lives, but you were protecting me from legal liability. This is an example of the *stasis* of quality, which is a stasis that refers to significance, or magnitude, or extenuating circumstances.

Before we completely leave this hypothetical car theft, let's consider one more example. I come up to you and I say, "You stole my car." You respond, "Hey don't accuse me of theft out here on the street. Theft is a criminal offense. If you've got a case, prosecute; I'll see you in court." Now what's at issue? I've made an assertion: "You stole my car." Your response essentially says, "This isn't the right place to discuss it. It's not the right forum, not the right procedure." This invokes what we call the *stasis* of place.

To recapitulate, in the classical understanding of the term *stasis,* we have stasis of conjecture, definition, quality, and place. At the risk of stating the obvious, notice how in these four examples, the nature of your response, together with my assertion, produced a very different point of clash: in one case, whether an act occurred; in another, what to call it; in another, whether it was justified; and in another, whether we're in the right place or the right forum in order to discuss it. It makes a difference which of these we pick because subsequent arguments need to be addressed to the focal point of controversy. If the focal point of controversy is what we call it, we don't want to spend our time arguing about whether it occurred. What's most important in determining stasis, the point of clash, is not the original assertion, but the response that's made to it.

After all, my assertion, "You stole my car," was the same in each case. What determined the different stases was how you responded to my assertion. You have choices in how you could reply. Some replies will be stronger; some replies will be weaker; but it's the reply to the assertion that has a lot to do with determining where the stasis is.

Does this mean that I as the original advocate have nothing to say about where the focal point of the controversy will be? No, because the original arguer, in determining what argument to advance in the first place, should realize different response possibilities. If the arguer wants the stasis to be at one place or at another place, he or she ought to try to frame the original assertion to produce that result. It's the response more than the original assertion that determines the focal point of the controversy. That's one thing to notice.

The second thing to notice is that, generally speaking, with one exception that I'll mention later, stasis is progressive. What I mean by that is, if we choose to have the dispute center on definition, we are implicitly conceding conjecture. If we choose to focus on quality, we are implicitly conceding both conjecture and definition.

Go back to my example. When you reply, "No I borrowed your car. I didn't steal it," you're implicitly conceding that you had possession of it. The question of whether you had possession or not, conjecture has been waived from the dispute. It's been effectively stipulated. When you say, "It's a good thing, because I used the car to take someone to the hospital," you're implicitly conceding both that you had it and that you stole it. You're saying that you stole it for good reason, but you stole it. And if you stole it, you had it. So stasis is progressive. Definition implicitly concedes conjecture. Quality implicitly concedes both conjecture and definition.

What does that mean? It means that if you're replying to my assertion, as a general rule, you want to reply that would a take a stasis as close to the beginning of the chain as you can carry it. So if, for example, you can carry the response that you never had my car at all, that ought to be what you say. Suppose there were 10 eyewitnesses who saw you in possession of my car; then it's pointless to say, "I never had your car." Not only is that an assertion that will quickly be shown to be false, but when it's shown to be false, it will cast doubt on your overall credibility. If you make one false claim, you might well make others. The idea is not necessarily to pick the first stasis; it's to pick to the first stasis that you are pretty confident you can sustain, because as you pick higher levels of stasis, you're implicitly conceding what came before.

Sometimes you can combine the stases. What if you said, "I never had your car, but if I had stolen it, it would have been for a good cause." There you're combining conjecture and quality, and sometimes that can work effectively. You've made one response contingent on the other. You said, "I never had your car"—that's the first response—"but if I took it, it would have been for a good cause."

On the other hand, sometimes the combination of stases can suggest that you're being evasive, that you're not really confident of your position. What if you said, "Hey I never had it, and if I had it I would have borrowed it, and if I stole it, it would have been for good cause." You're putting a number of these together, and the natural kind of psychological response is, "Methinks you doth protest too much," And your whole credibility is called into question.

So far, we've seen that the response to the assertion largely governs the *stasis*, and that *stasis* generally is progressive. I said there is one exception to that. That is, that *stasis* in place is usually preemptive of everything else. What do I mean when I say that? If we're not in the right place to discuss this question, if we're not employing the right procedure or the right forum, then the substance of the dispute— whether this happened or not, what we call it, whether it was justified—that really doesn't matter until we get ourselves in the right forum; so that when you reply to me, "Don't bring this accusation on the street. I'll see you in court," what you're saying, in effect, is, "Don't even begin talking about conjecture, or definition, or quality until we get into the right place." Thus, *stasis* in place tends to be preemptive.

By the way, this is why we often will find arguments about process or procedure used in situations to trump arguments about the substance of the case.

That's the basic idea of stasis. I think we can see almost intuitively why it's such a useful tool. It reminds us that there are multiple possible points of controversy; multiple points of stasis; multiple focal points determined by the joining of an assertion and the response to the assertion. In order for the controversy to proceed, we need to identify the precise point of clash and then to invite the advocates to respond to it.

So far, I've used a simple example, and we have a simple understanding of stasis. You may have noticed that I used a legal example, because I said the concept originally developed for purposes of application to law courts. It has a broader application, a broader focus than that. It can be applied to disputes of other kinds as well, although we have to complicate our understanding a little bit in order to do so.

I want to do that by talking about how stasis applies to resolutions of policy, because these are probably the most complex resolutions; and so, if we can see it there, then of course, we can see it anywhere.

Let's look at how stasis applies on resolutions of policy. Here's why they are more complicated than legal questions, because multiple issues will be at play and each issue will have its own stasis. We saw this when we talked about Colin Powell's speech, where many issues were discussed at the same time. We said that the kinds of issues, the *topoi*, that policy resolutions addressed are things like the following: Is there a problem? Where is credit or blame due? Will the proposal solve the problem? On balance, is the proposal going to leave us better off? All of those issues will be discussed.

For example, let's go back to the case of national missile defense systems. One of the issues is, "Is there anything wrong with our current defense policy?" In the course of discussing national missile defense, I might say, "We've left ourselves vulnerable to terrorist threats." You might respond, "The threat of terrorism by this means is minimal." When you do that, you've invoked a stasis of quality. You see, you've not denied that the problem exists; you've not denied that it ought to be called a threat; but you've said it's minimal. It's not that serious. It's not serious enough to really worry about.

On the issue of, "Is there a problem?" this dispute might center on the stasis of quality. But I said another issue was, "Can the proposal solve the problem?" On this one you might say, "Hey this is fantasy land. The technology for national missile defense doesn't even exist." What you're saying is that on that issue, there is no solution. The stasis would focus on conjecture. You say, "No solution exists; never mind whether we really call it national missile defense, or how much of the problem is solved; it's not even there." The stasis is in conjecture.

At the same time we're discussing both of those issues, another issue is, "Do the costs exceed the benefits?" On this one you might say, "It costs too much." I might reply, "But you know, those aren't real costs because you've got to compare them to the cost of doing nothing. So net, they're not real costs of building this system." On this one you see the stasis is in definition. We're not disputing what the costs are. We're disputing whether they should really be called costs. We've got this one controversy: should we build a national missile defense system; and in talking about that, here we are facing multiple issues with different points of stasis all at the same time.

We can quickly see, I think, why a policy resolution is more complicated than a legal question. Multiple issues are at play, each with its own stasis. However, stasis in place is usually not applicable to policy resolutions, because resolutions are subjects for general deliberation about what we should do. Pretty much whatever forum we use to talk about what we should do is okay. It's just as appropriate for you and me to talk about national missile defense as it for members of Congress; or for scientists; or for members of the national administration. Usually in a policy controversy, stasis in place is pretty much irrelevant.

What does that leave us with? It leaves us with the four *topoi:* Is there a problem? Who's to blame? Will the proposal work? And, on balance, are we better off?—each of which could have a stasis of conjecture, or definition, or quality. For those of you who are into matrix analysis, you can see what this gives us is a four by three matrix. Down one side you can imagine the *topoi*, and across the top you can imagine the possible points of stasis.

Let's do that as an exercise for just a minute. For convenience's sake, I'm going to shorthand the *topoi*, the issue categories, as ill, blame, cure, and cost. Ill, of course, is, "Is there a problem?" Blame, "Where's the responsibility?" Cure, "Is there a solution?" Cost, "On balance, are we better off?" We have ill, blame, cure, and cost. Then we have conjecture, definition, and quality. Let's see how this might work.

I'm going to consider a new example, that the federal government should establish a patient's bill of rights to regulate medical care. Let's take the *topoi* and see how we could have different possible stases. First of all, ill: Do the practices of health maintenance organizations, HMOs, leave patients unsatisfied? That's a question of conjecture. Should this dissatisfaction be considered a violation of their rights?—definition. Is the violation great enough that something should be done about it as a matter of public policy?—quality.

Now just on this question, "Is there a problem?" you can see how picking one stasis or another will make a huge difference to the way the controversy proceeds. If you say in response to my assertion, "There are no serious problems with HMOs. Patients are satisfied with the care they receive," then we talk about one set of questions, conjectural questions. If you say, "Well, patients might be satisfied or dissatisfied just like customers in any case are satisfied or dissatisfied; but a dissatisfied person doesn't mean that rights have been violated." Now we're talking about what we call this dissatisfaction. If you reply, "Well, you know there may be some infringements on rights here and there. No system is perfect, but it's not great enough that we should invoke the federal government and public policy to do something about it," then we're talking about matters of significance—not about whether there's a problem, not about what to call it, but how great the problem is. On this issue of ill, we have all these possibilities opened up; and, of course, if I imagine one stasis and you imagine a different one, we're going to have a mismatched argument.

Now let's look at the question of blame, the second issue category. Do HMOs make the key medical decisions?—a question of conjecture. Is their discretion abused?—a question of definition. Should we consider any aggravating or mitigating circumstances?—a question of quality, just like in the "you stole my car example," where we said there were mitigating circumstances. Here at this level, too, there are different ways to focus the argument.

Look at the category of cure. This is the issue category that asks, will the proposal solve the problem? Can a bill of rights be devised? Can we imagine a solution?—conjecture. Will it work? Will it correct for the violations of rights?—definition. How much of the abuse of HMOs will it really address, and how much will be left?—quality that deals with significance or degree. Here again on this issue, we have multiple possible points of stasis.

Finally, look at the *topos*—that's the singular of *topoi*. Look at the issue category of cost. What will a bill of rights cost patients? How much will it increase their medical care expense?—a question of conjecture. Are they real costs compared to the costs of doing nothing?—definition. Are the costs worth it? Is it worth it for us to bring about this result? Do the benefits outweigh the costs?—a question of quality.

Look what we did in this relatively simple example. We took this imaginary four-by-three matrix and we said, "Okay, if we're going to discuss the question of a patient's bill of rights, we could have as many as 12 different points of stasis in that controversy." We had four categories of issues, and on each issue we had three possible stases. Now you wonder why the discussion of topics like a patient's bill of rights, or national missile defense, or educational policy, is so complicated. It's because multiple stasis are at play at the same time. Moreover, the participants in the argumentative exchanges may not be on the same wavelength. They may not be addressing the same stasis at the same time.

Let me be very clear. I'm not suggesting that an advocate ought to raise all 12 of these points of clash in talking about a matter of public policy. Indeed, the effect of doing that would be about the same as the effect of my saying, "Hey, I didn't I have your car, and if I had I would have borrowed it; and if I stole it, it would have been a good thing. And by the way, don't speak about it here." It would suggest evasiveness. It would suggest not coming to grips with the issue.

The purpose of talking about the whole matrix is not for us to pick all 12 points—we generally pick no more than one on any given issue—but it's to make us aware of the range of choices that exists about what shape a controversy could take, based upon on how you respond to the assertions that I might make. What I've tried to suggest here is that this concept that was originally developed for law courts—where it's relatively easy to apply because there are formal rules in a law court that determine a procedure, that determine what's relevant and not relevant—actually can be taken and applied more broadly to disputes about policy. If it can be applied to disputes about policy, I hope we can see, with a little bit of imagination, how it can also be applied to disputes about value, disputes about definition, and disputes about fact.

Now, since you've borne with me as I've explained the concept, let me address the question of why this is such an important concept. To do this, let's imagine the negative. What happens when the advocates in a controversy fail to agree on the point of stasis? What happens when they don't address the same point? Sometimes it can result in the loss of the argument.

Many of you are familiar with the very famous Scopes trial that took place in 1925 that came about when a biology teacher named John Scopes taught the theory of evolution in violation of a Tennessee state law that made it a crime to do so. In the course of the trial of Mr. Scopes, the defense, represented by Clarence Darrow, argued that the theory of evolution was true and, therefore, it was okay for Scopes to teach it. The prosecution argued that the teaching of evolution was unlawful; therefore, Scopes violated the law.

Let's think about the stasis categories. Neither side is disputing conjecture; there's no question that this happened. The prosecution is arguing definition: "this act was unlawful," while the defense is arguing quality: "it's okay because the theory is true." The prosecution replies, "We don't care whether the theory is true. The state has a right to prohibit this teaching and, therefore, Scopes broke the law." Remember, we said that stasis is progressive. Quality concedes definition and conjecture; so according to this analysis, the defense, by picking stasis in quality, has implicitly conceded all the prosecution needed to prove in order to win the case. The argument is that faulty choice of stasis doomed the case. There is a competing analysis, by the way, that says the defense wasn't trying to win the case; they were trying to build a record on appeal. But that's another matter.

Sometimes failing to agree on the stasis can hijack the argument and change understanding of what it is. For example, in the dispute in 2005 about Social Security reform, Some advocates picked as their stasis point, "Will private retirement accounts solve the problem?" They didn't get very far in the pubic dialogue because the public was focused on the question, "Is there a problem?" So it was a faulty analysis of stasis. Sometimes it can produce a stalemate, as in the abortion dispute, when one side is arguing that abortion is wrong, and the other side is arguing the question of who can decide whether or not to have this procedure in a particular circumstance. There's no agreement on stasis and, hence, no clash. Developing clash that is meaningful, productive, and responsive to the argument depends first of all on selecting the appropriate stasis. How else it occurs is what we will focus on in the next lecture.

Lecture Nine
Attack and Defense I

Scope:

This and the following lecture will consider the processes of refuting and rebuilding cases. Despite the seeming use of a military metaphor, attacks on a case serve the cooperative purpose of reaching the best possible resolution of a controversy. Just as choices were involved in constructing the case, so are decisions to be made in planning an attack. These include which arguments to attack, at which parts of the argument to focus the attack, and what type of attack to develop. These choices often are made instinctively by skilled arguers, but they can be understood better if they are examined systematically.

Outline

I. The dynamics of controversy involve what happens after a case is presented.

    A. Assuming that the case is plausible on its face, its presentation obligates other arguers either to accept it or to meet the burden of rejoinder.

    B. The burden of rejoinder is met through the interrelated processes of attack and defense, together referred to as *refutation.*

    C. We should not be misled by the military metaphor in thinking about attack and defense.

        1. The goal of arriving at sound judgment is shared.

        2. If well conducted, attack and defense are constructive processes and both parties benefit from the exchange.

        3. What attack and defense in argumentation do share with military campaigns is concern for strategic choices and for making them carefully.

II. Attacking arguments involves several selection choices.

    A. Which arguments to attack?

        1. Not every argument requires attack.

        2. Attacking every argument can involve one in tenuous situations or create internal inconsistencies.

3. Arguments not attacked may be either ignored or granted.
4. Deciding what to attack helps to narrow the potential issues to the actual issues.
5. As with case construction, the strength of the attack and the relevance of the argument to the resolution should govern the decision.

B. Which part of the argument to attack?
1. One option is to attack the claim, by denying it outright or by countering it.
2. One option is to attack the evidence on which the claim is based.
3. One option is to attack the inference linking evidence to claim.
4. One option is to attack the contextual assumptions that undergird the whole argument.
5. The choice should be governed by what will give the most result with the least effort (the mini-max principle).

C. What type of attack to develop?
1. Asking a question is basically a holding operation that can be nullified when the answer is given, unless the question is unanswerable.
2. Identifying internal deficiencies in the argument will show how the arguer failed to meet the burden of proof.
3. Identifying inconsistencies in the argument can cast doubt on the sincerity of the arguer, as well as requiring a response to the inconsistency.
4. Labeling the opponent's argument strategy can identify fallacies or attempts to thwart the goal of critical reasoning and resolving disagreement.
5. Using a counterargument is a denial of the claim itself, defining a point of *stasis,* and forcing the listener to choose between competing claims.
6. Recontextualizing the argument will place it in a broader context in which it now appears unsatisfactory.

D. Although arguers often make these choices instinctively and in the heat of the moment, studying them systematically helps to make us aware of the range of choices and to "coach" better strategic judgments.

III. A selection from the Kennedy-Nixon debates of 1960 helps to illustrate these selection choices.

    A. There was much substantive argument in the Kennedy-Nixon debates, as in this example about the size of the federal budget.

    B. Nixon's argument, as presented by the panelist, was that the cost of Kennedy's program would exceed that of his own by $10 billion dollars a year.

    C. Kennedy makes several choices about how to attack this argument.

        1. He recontextualizes it as an argument about whether the budget is in balance.

        2. He provides counterarguments showing examples where his budget will cost less than Nixon's.

        3. He acknowledges that he will spend more on education and defense, implying that these increases are desirable.

        4. He accuses Nixon of misstating his figures in reaching the conclusion that his budget will cost $10 billion more than Nixon's.

    D. These choices reflect Kennedy's application of the mini-max principle; we can consider whether he made the best strategic choices.

Essential Reading:

Austin J. Freeley and David L. Steinberg, *Argumentation and Debate: Critical Thinking for Reasoned Decision Making*, chapter 14.

Richard D. Rieke and Malcolm O. Sillars, *Argumentation and Critical Decision Making*, pp. 225–248.

Supplementary Reading:

J. W. Patterson and David Zarefsky, *Contemporary Debate*, pp. 70–85.

Questions to Consider:

1. What skills and attitudes are necessary for the attack on an argument to achieve its constructive potential and contribute to the goals of all arguers to resolve disagreement?

2. Under what circumstances will each of the various types of attack (asking questions, identifying internal deficiencies, and so on) be the most effective choice?

Lecture Nine—Transcript
Attack and Defense I

Hello again. It's good to be back. Two lectures ago, when we were talking about case construction, I used the term prima facie meaning "on first face." I said one of the things that we want to do when we put a case together is to have it be prima facie, meaning that upon first hearing it, it will seem reasonable, and plausible, and it will support the resolution that we're trying to advance. Assuming that somebody has done that, then the other arguer is in a position where he or she either needs to accept the case or respond to it; and coming up with a response to the case is called meeting the burden of rejoinder.

Last time, we talked about how one begins to meet that burden of rejoinder by identifying the stasis, the focal point of the case, so that we can know exactly what's in controversy. Then, we can either respond to that point or, if we want to relocate the controversy, we can do that; but at least we can understand where it centers. That brings us to a study of the dynamics of controversy—what happens after the case has been presented and somebody is ready to respond to it.

Meeting the burden of rejoinder is accomplished through the interrelated process of attack and defense, which together are known as refutation. Refutation is sometimes defined as, "planning an execution of attacks and defenses as part of the testing and evaluation of arguments." The next two lectures will be devoted to attack and defense, to refutation.

There are two problems that I want to address right off the bat, before we get into the heart of this material. One is that, for some people, talking about attack and defense is difficult because it sounds like it's a military metaphor, and it sounds like what we're trying to do is overwhelm, or vanquish, or utterly defeat an opponent. Remember what we've said throughout these lectures: that's not what argumentation is all about. The goal of arriving at a sound judgment is a goal that the arguers share. They're in this together. The purpose of mobilizing a strong attack and coming up with a strong defense is to give arguments a rigorous test, so that we'll have confidence in the results. Indeed, if they're well conducted, attack and defense are constructive exercises, and both parties should benefit from the exchange. If there is an aspect of the military metaphor that's appropriate, it's the notion of strategic planning, careful analysis, concern for choice, and for making those choices carefully; and I hope we'll see how that's done in these next two lectures.

The other problem I want to speak to you briefly about is that the things that we're going to talk about in a highly systematic way are things that are often done instinctively, almost intuitively, in an actual argument. We're going to lay out a series of steps and questions that in most cases, in an actual argument, arguers don't stop, hold everything, and ask themselves. You might wonder why we're going to subject this process to such scrutiny, and the answer is simple. We're trying to learn a series of skills. These are skills, which, if we understand them, we can practice them, and we can refine them, and get ourselves into a position where, when we engage in arguments, we'll be more likely to do it naturally and instinctively; but we have to start off understanding what it is that we're doing.

I also want to alert you that there is far more to say about attack than about defense; so the two lectures won't be evenly divided. As we'll see, many of the options of the defense are constrained by the nature of the attack.

Let's begin with attacks. When we want to respond to a case, to attack a case, there's a series of strategic choices that we have to make. They involve both selection and arrangement, just as case construction involves both selection and arrangement choices. I want to begin now with selection choices, and I want to focus most of our time in this lecture on four of these choices. The first one is, which arguments to attack? Remember back in Lecture 6, when we talked about Colin Powell at the UN Security Council, and we had a fairly elaborate diagram of his case, and there were lots of different arguments in it at varying levels. We don't need, if we're going to attack his case, to attack every single argument. In fact, if we did, we would get so bogged down in the attacks that we might lose track of what the case was all about.

Moreover, if we tried to attack every argument in a case, we can find ourselves unknowingly in an inconsistent position where the other person can respond and knock out some of our attacks. For example, also in Lecture 6, we talked about a set of arguments involving airline travel. At one point, I said it was really difficult to understand airline pricing. At another point, I said the ticket agents and reservation agents are not terribly helpful. Suppose you wanted to attack both of those arguments. You might say, "First of all, airline pricing is really pretty simple. There aren't all of these difficulties and complexities, so I don't know what you're even talking about advancing the argument." Then you get to the one about ticket agents and you say, "You know, these ticket agents and reservation clerks are really helpful and they work out all the difficulties in the pricing." But wait, the first attack says there aren't difficulties in pricing. The second attack says they work out the difficulties. The person who makes the original argument could respond to these two attacks by saying, "These attacks work at cross purposes; throw them both out."

Thus, we want to think carefully about which arguments to attack. Besides, some arguments might not even need attacking; they may not matter that much. Even if you give them up, you haven't lost much; and if you attack and defeat them, you haven't gained much. For example, suppose someone says, "Airports have become much more crowded in the years since September 11, 2001." And you respond by saying, "They're less crowded in 2005 than they were in 2004." Suppose you're right? What have you gained? You haven't defeated the argument that crowding has increased since 2001. Suppose you let it go; what difference does it make if you have other arguments that are going to deal with the causes of crowding, or are going to present ways to relieve crowding? Not every argument needs to be attacked; and if it's not attacked, it can either be ignored or it can be acknowledged and granted, often with a flourish in which you say, "This is an argument that does us no damage. It doesn't make any difference."

Deciding which arguments to attack helps to narrow down the potential issues in the case to the actual issues. How do you decide which arguments to attack? You use exactly the same criteria that you used when deciding what arguments to put in the case. Are they strong?—which means, will the audience be likely to believe the evidence that the attack is based on? And, is the relevance of the attack to defeating the argument high? These are the same criteria that ought to govern making that decision. The first decision is which arguments to attack. The second key decision is which part of the argument to attack? Now I want to refer you back to Lecture 5, where we had a diagram of a simple argument that had a claim; it had evidence; and it had an inference linking the two. One could choose to attack the argument, once you've decided which argument to attack, at any one of those points or at more than one of those points.

One option is to attack the claim by denying it outright or by offering some sort of counterclaim. The claim in the argument is, "Airline delays have increased." We might deny that outright and attack it by saying, "No, airline delays have not increased." We've denied the claim, and if you remember from our stasis discussion, that focuses stasis in conjecture. Has it happened? Have delays increased? Or we might counter the claim, not by denying it outright, but by saying for instance, "Increased delays are really a minor problem," in which case we focused stasis on definition. Is it a problem? Or increased delays are justified by safety considerations, in which case we focused stasis in quality. One option, then, is to deny the claim outright or to counter it.

However, that's not the only option. It may not be the claim that we want to attack. Another way to attack an argument is to attack the evidence on which the claim is based. We might say, "You've talked about airport crowding, but you've really examined a limited sample of airports. You've only talked about Chicago O'Hare, L.A. International, and Washington Dulles. We know that those happen to be three of the most crowded airports in the country; so your evidence really doesn't establish that airport crowding is a significant problem overall."

We might say, "Your evidence comes from an unqualified or a biased source. You quoted an occasional tourist. A tourist doesn't have enough experience with airports to really evaluate whether they're crowded or not."

We might say, "You quoted a known critic of the airline industry. Of course that person is going to find faults with every aspect of the industry that he or she could." It's an unqualified source or a biased source. Any of these examples illustrate attacking the evidence. Remember, because we said the evidence has to be agreed to for the argument to get anywhere, you've attacked the argument by attacking that part of it.

You might choose to attack the inference, to attack the link between the evidence and the claim. You're not attacking either one directly, but you're attacking the vital connection between the two. For example you might say, "The relationship between crowded airplanes and rude passengers is only a correlation. You haven't shown that one causes the other."

You might say, "You've said the planes are crowded; that just means that they're not flying enough planes. If they increased the schedule, it would solve that problem. What's true of one plane wouldn't be true of all." You might say, "You've drawn an analogy to what happened after airline deregulation in the 1970s, but that's a false analogy."

I realize we haven't yet talked in any detail about specific inferences. We'll be doing that a few lectures from now. For now, just remember that attacking the link, attacking the inference, is just as strong a way to undercut the argument as is attacking the claim or the evidence.

There's one more choice you could make about which part of the argument to attack. Think back to that diagram that had the evidence, the claim, and the inference. Now, imagine that we enclose that entire diagram in a box. We have a box drawn around it, and that box represents the underlying context of the argument—the set of assumptions, the framework in which the argument is based. You might choose to attack that.

For example you might say, "This whole argument about airline crowding, and airports, and unpleasantness is based on the assumption that the convenience of the consumer is the principal goal of the airline industry. While obviously they're concerned with consumers, it's far more important to focus on safety, on the perseveration of life, and on avoiding threats to national security. If we look at the airline industry and the situation of airports in that context, then we get a whole different light on the matter, and these concerns appear relatively trivial." What we've done in that example is, we've responded not to the claim, the evidence, or the inference, but to the whole framework of assumptions that surrounds the argument.

Once we've decided which arguments to attack out of that whole case, for each one we attack, we further choose whether to go after the evidence, the claim, the inference, or the underlying context. We could, of course, choose to go after more than one, if there's good reason to do so. The choice of which parts to attack, and how many parts to attack should be governed by a very simple principal: what will get us the most effective result in bringing the argument into question with the least expenditure of time and effort and energy? We might think of this as a *minimax* kind of principle, to use a term that economists sometimes use. What, with minimum effort, will get the maximum gain? That will help us choose what part of the argument to attack.

So, we have which arguments to attack, what part of the argument to attack, and the third choice is what type of attack to develop. Here, at the risk of seeming to split hairs, I want to make sure that we all realize that there are lots of different ways to attack an argument. For example, one could ask a question about an argument: "You said that airports have delays. How many airports have these delays?" This is generally not a good attack strategy, and the reason is that it doesn't build up any kind of equity for you. Once the question is answered, you have nothing left. The original argument is back there again in full.

The only time when I would normally advise attacking an argument by asking a question is when the question is important to the argument and is unanswerable. For instance, suppose that, as one part of the case, somebody said, "The airline industry executives are meeting together in secret and planning how to curtail their routes." You say, "Where's the evidence that they're having these secret meetings?" The person responds, "Well, they met last year in Detroit, and they met in New York." "Wait a minute; we know about those meetings, they're not secret. What about all these secret meetings that you're referring to?" Of course, by the nature of secrecy, you don't know, and so you can't answer the question; and yet the question is important to the case. With that exception, asking a question is generally not a very good way to attack a case.

Here are some other possibilities: identifying internal deficiencies in the argument will show how the arguer failed to meet his or her burden of proof, if you show problems with the evidence or problems with the inference, as in the examples that I've mentioned before. A third way to attack an argument is to identify inconsistencies in the argument that can cast doubt on the sincerity of the arguer, as well as requiring a response to the inconsistency.

For instance, let's suppose that you're responding to an argument that refers to delays, and you've suggested, "Scheduling changes can reduce airline delays;" then later on, you've suggested that, "Take-off and landing restrictions can reduce airport congestion"—two different problems that have been identified in the case. Wait a minute, scheduling changes would supposedly reduce delays, but take-off and landing restrictions, while they cut congestion, would increase delays. You could point out that, here's an argument that's working at cross purposes with itself. As we saw in an earlier lecture, when you identify an inconsistency, logically, that means only that one of those claims must be false; but psychologically, it casts doubt on the sincerity of both claims, and on the credibility of the arguer, him or herself. That's another way to attack an argument.

Yet another way is to label the opponent's argument strategy. This approach relies on the principal that, once you identify the underlying strategy, you reduce the effectiveness of that very strategy; because you've called attention to it, you've recognized it for what it is. If you respond to argument by saying, "That's loaded language," you've identified the strategy that the arguer is doing, which is to load the deck by using language that is not neutral, that is biased language. That calls attention to it.

You might say, "You're trying to create a dilemma where there really isn't a dilemma. We're not forced into these two undesirable choices in the way that you thought." What you're doing is, you're pointing out attempts to thwart the goal of reasoning critically and resolving the underlying disagreement.

Those are four ways you can attack an argument. Another is a counter-argument. This is a denial of the claim itself, as in the examples I illustrated above. When you do that, the nature of your denial will define the point of stasis, and now the listener will have to choose between the competing claims that you and your opponent have advanced.

Finally, the sixth choice that I want to mention: you could choose to contextualize the argument, placing it in a broader context in which it appears to be unsatisfactory. My example before, when I tried to re-contextualize from consumer convenience to safety and national security, is a good example of that. Thus, just as in deciding which arguments to attack, and which parts of the argument to attack, an important strategic choice is what type of attack to develop.

There's one more choice I want to mention very briefly, and that's how many attacks to develop. Given all of the arguments in Colin Powell's case, if you want to attack it, how many attacks should you make? The reason that I want to cover this so quickly is that the answer is exactly the same as it was when we discussed this topic under case construction— how many arguments to put in the case. We can increase the amplitude of the attack—that is, a wider range, more attacks—by hedging our bets. The individual attacks may not be conclusive, and so we'll put a lot of them together and we'll convince some people that that argument's weak for this reason, and some people for this reason, and some people for this reason. That takes advantage of the fact that the audience is heterogeneous. Different people will be appealed to by different kinds of attacks.

But if we increase the amplitude and have lots of attacks we might weaken our credibility. It may seem like we're just launching these scatter-shot attacks here, and here, and here, because we don't have anything really substantial to say against the case; and we run the risk of getting ourselves into an inconsistent position, suggesting that we don't have confidence in our own attacks. Just as we said with respect to case construction, we have to find the right balance between too few and too many attacks, based upon the specifics of the case and of what we want to accomplish.

These, then, are the four basic choices that relate to selection when we go about attacking a case: deciding which arguments to attack, where in the argument, what type of attack, how many attacks. As I've said, arguers often make these choices instinctively and in the heat of the moment. But we want to study them systematically so that we can understand them, so that we can become aware of the range of choices, and begin to coach ourselves in how to make better judgments and better choices.

Lest you think that this is all a hypothetical discussion and all grounded in theory, I want to spend a few minutes with an actual example of choices regarding selection of attacks. For this purpose, I want to go back to the very first presidential debates between John F. Kennedy and Richard Nixon in 1960.

So much of what we remember about presidential debates is either the mistakes or the gaffes that get made, or the visual contrast between the candidates, that we focus sometimes on superficial things, and don't realize that there's actually a lot of substantial argument going on. That was certainly true in the Kennedy-Nixon debates. As an example, I want to pick what was not one of the major themes of the debates by any means, but what came up during the course of the third debate.

You may remember that the format was that there were questions posed by journalists, and one candidate had two-and-a-half minutes to answer, and then the other candidate had a shorter time in which to respond. Sometimes the journalists posed open-ended questions, so that the candidate's response was the case construction, and the other candidate was making the attack; but sometimes the journalists focused a question on an argument that the opposing candidate had been making, so that the candidate to whom the question was posed was invited to attack that argument.

That's what happened in this example, when the journalist Douglas Kater asked Senator Kennedy this question: "Vice President Nixon says that he has cost the two party platforms and that yours would run at least $10 billion a year more than his. You have denied his figures. He has called on you to supply your figures. Would you do that?" So Kater has posed Nixon's argument and has invited Kennedy to respond to that argument. Look at the selection choices that Kennedy makes in what he says. In the course of his two-and-a-half minutes, he basically says four things. He says, "Yes I have stated in both debates, and state again, that I believe in a balanced budget, and have supported that concept during my 14 years in the Congress. The only two times when an unbalanced budget is warranted would be during a serious recession or a national emergency."

The first thing that Kennedy does is to re-contextualize the argument. He does not talk about whether his program will cost $10 billion more than Nixon's; he doesn't want to focus on that. He wants to focus on the question of whether he is fiscally responsible. His reasoning is, "Most people that argue that you're spending too much really mean to say that you're fiscally irresponsible." He selects a stasis in quality, saying that costing more is okay because the budget is balanced. He re-contextualizes the argument.

The second thing he says is, "On the question of the cost of our budget, I have stated that it's my best judgment that our agricultural program will cost $1.5 billion, possibly $2 billion less than the present. My judgment is that the vice president's program will cost $1 billion more than the present. Second, I believe that the high interest rate policy that this administration has followed has added about $3 billion a year to interest on the debt. I would hope under a different monetary policy we could reduce that burden. Third, I think it's possible to gain $700 million to $1 billion through tax changes, which I believe would close up loopholes. Fourth, I have suggested that medical care for the aged would be paid under Social Security,"—which, by the way, at the time was off budget; it was not part of the federal budget.

What Kennedy does is, he identifies these four specific examples where he thinks his program would cost less than Nixon's would cost, inviting you perhaps to generalize that his program overall would call less, but not directly responding to the claim that his program would cost $10 billion more. He's attacked evidence in this second case. He has attacked specific examples.

Third, he acknowledges that in some areas he will spend more than Nixon. He says, "In my judgment we would spend more money on aid to education. We'd spend more money on housing. We'd spend more money, and I hope more wisely on defense than this administration has." In those areas, he's granting the argument. He's choosing not to attack the argument with respect to those examples, because he's going to suggest it's a good thing to spend more there.

Finally, he accuses Nixon of misstating his figures. "Mr. Nixon misstates my figures constantly, which is, of course, his right; but the fact of the matter is, here is where I stand, and I just want to have it on the public record." Again he's attacking evidence.

These choices about what to do reflect Kennedy's application of the minimax principle. He thinks, here is where, with minimum effort, he can get the best results in launching his attack. We can see what he does and doesn't do, and can evaluate his choices based on the understanding that we've just gained about what the advocate's range of choices are. Next time, we'll look at attack choices that relate to arrangement, and then we'll talk about defense.

Lecture Ten
Attack and Defense II

Scope:

This lecture continues the discussion of attacking arguments by focusing on a second set of choices: those related to the arrangement and presentation of the attacks. Then the focus shifts to defending and rebuilding arguments. The choices available to the defense are more limited. The lecture will consider the basic strategic options of the defense, then highlight the most significant selection and arrangement choices. The lecture also will consider a group of general methods of refutation, argument techniques that are available to both attackers and defenders. Finally, the lecture will consider how the pattern of attacks and defenses, responses, and extensions helps to move the dispute forward by narrowing the areas of dispute and helping the arguers to find common ground.

Outline

I.   Attacking arguments involves several arrangement choices.
  A. Should the attacks be organized in the same way as the arguments being attacked?
    1. Doing so will make it easier for audiences to follow the argument.
    2. But doing so may put the respondent on the opponent's ground.
    3. Building one's own organizational scheme around the central points in dispute may be more effective.
    4. In the example of the Kennedy-Nixon debates in Lecture Nine, notice that Kennedy developed his own organization.
  B. How completely should the attack be developed?
    1. The argument being attacked should be stated in a way that the audience will accept.
    2. The basis of the attack should be clearly stated.
    3. The attack should be developed and supported.
    4. The significance of what the attack has accomplished should be made clear.

5. Notice that in the Kennedy-Nixon debate example, Kennedy omits some of these steps in the apparent belief that they will be obvious to the audience.

II. Strategic choices regarding the defense of an argument that has been attacked are more limited.

A. The basic strategic options are few.

    1. One can demonstrate that the attack is inapplicable to the case.

    2. One can demonstrate that the attack is of trivial consequence.

    3. One can demonstrate that the attack is inadequately established.

    4. One can demonstrate that the attack is in error.

    5. The most basic choices, however, are made in the original presentation of the argument, that is, taking possible attacks into account and considering how to reduce their impact.

B. The selection choice is not whether to respond to the attack (for that could be fatal) but how seriously to take the attack and which of the above response strategies to use.

C. The arrangement choice is whether the structure of the original argument or the structure of the attack will be the dominant organizational plan.

    1. The respondent should be careful not just to repeat the original argument without extending it or responding to the attack.

    2. The respondent should be careful not to let the attack "run away with" the argument so that the attack, rather than the argument, becomes the dominant focus.

III. The 1960 Kennedy-Nixon debates also illustrate strategic choices related to the defense.

A. Remember that the original argument was that Kennedy's platform would cost more than Nixon's and that Kennedy attacked the argument by recontextualizing it, providing counterexamples, admitting some increases, and challenging Nixon's figures.

B. Nixon makes various choices in defending his original argument.

1. He denies that he is misstating Kennedy's figures.
2. He labels Kennedy's counterexamples and says that they are illusory.
3. He denies some of the counterexamples or suggests that they are worse.

C. Notice that Nixon neither follows Kennedy's exact order nor returns to his original argument; this is a questionable choice.

IV. General methods of refutation can be used in both attack and defense.

A. *Reductio ad absurdum* suggests that the other arguer's position leads to unacceptable implications.

B. Turning the tables shows how a position claimed by one party actually benefits the other.

C. Dilemmas suggest that the opposing arguer must choose between unattractive alternatives.

D. Argument from residues dictates the opponent's position by eliminating all other possibilities.

E. Argument *a fortiori* suggests that what is true of the lesser is true of the greater, or vice versa.

F. Contradictions and inconsistencies eliminate at least one of the other arguer's positions, as well as questioning the other arguer's general credibility.

V. The processes of attack and defense together help to move the discussion forward.

A. Strategic choices made by the individual arguers will waive some potential issues from consideration.

B. Some aspects of the controversy will be settled or dropped through attack and defense.

C. The central issues on which the dispute turns will be identified, the positions of the arguers will be clarified, and the differences between them will be recognized.

Essential Reading:

Austin J. Freeley and David L. Steinberg, *Argumentation and Debate: Critical Thinking for Reasoned Decision Making*, chapter 14.

Richard D. Rieke and Malcolm O. Sillars, *Argumentation and Critical Decision Making*, pp. 225–248.

Supplementary Reading:

J. W. Patterson and David Zarefsky, *Contemporary Debate*, pp. 70–85.

Questions to Consider:

1. How can one devise arguments that will take into account possible attacks and thereby minimize the need for substantial defense later?

2. Is the military metaphor (attack and defense) the best way to describe the processes of refuting and rebuilding cases? What are its implications? Is there a better alternative characterization of these processes?

Lecture Ten—Transcript
Attack and Defense II

It's good to be back. Last time we began a discussion of attack and defense, which, as I reminded us, are not military operations but constructive exercises in which we try to test arguments and reach conclusions, with which we're comfortable and in which we're confident. I talked about a number of choices regarding the selection of arguments to attack, and I said that there were also choices to be made with respect to arrangement. I want to pick up with that now and focus on two major arrangement choices.

The first of them is this question: Should the attacks be organized in the same way as the arguments that are being attacked? In other words, if the person that you're responding to presented a series of arguments—one, two, three, and four—and you're going to attack them, should you organize your attack the same way—one, two, three, and four? Doing so will make it easier for audiences to follow the argument; they follow the attack that's in exactly the same sequence and the same progression as the original argument. But, the danger is that doing so may put you on the opponent's ground. You may actually be better off building your own organizational scheme around what you think are the central points in the dispute.

Let me illustrate this with a fairly simple example. In Lecture 6, when I first began talking about airlines and airports and all of that, I used as one of my organizational examples a set of arguments in a series structure. Remember, I said my luggage was misdirected; it was mis-tagged when I checked it in at the airport. It went to the wrong city; and because it went to the wrong city, there were valuable documents that were missing; and because those were missing, I gave a presentation that was nowhere near as good as it should have been; and because my presentation wasn't very good, I got fired from my job. That was the whole series structure.

If you were going to attack that point by point, following the same organizational pattern that I used, you would take each one of the steps in the sequence that I developed; and if you were going to say something about it you'd say it, and if not you'd skip over it; but you would follow my structure. But doing that focuses the argument on my ground. What am I trying to do with that argument? I'm clearly trying to fix the responsibility for my losing my job on a series of mishaps that were ultimately caused by the airline.

Suppose, instead, you respond to this argument in a different way. Suppose you say, "Your termination notice was written before you ever left on this trip." That's all you say. Look, you haven't responded to my substructure; you haven't taken each one of these individual steps that I went through; but you have focused the dispute on the question, is it the airline's fault? You could well reason that that's the central question in the dispute, and if you can demonstrate that it's not the airline's fault, then you've defeated my argument, even though you haven't followed my substructure. This is because, if I was effectively fired before I ever started on this unfortunate trip, then it's pretty hard to argue that the airlines were responsible for whatever mishap befell me. What you've done is to focus on the conclusion you want to accomplish, which is that the responsibility doesn't lie with airline. What I'm trying suggest is that sometimes it makes sense to follow the organizational structure of the argument being attacked, but sometimes it doesn't. This is a choice to make, and it's a choice to make based on the strategic considerations of what you're trying to gain and what the argument looks like.

In the last lecture, I talked about the example of the Kennedy-Nixon debates. Kennedy developed his own organizational structure. He didn't follow along the lines that the questions suggested. Doing that enabled him to refocus the debate on what he wanted to emphasize, which was number one, that he was fiscally responsible; and number two, that he had good budget priorities. He wouldn't have been able to do that as effectively if he had responded directly, saying, for example: "You say my programs cost $10 billion more. No they don't. Here's the arithmetic piece, by piece, by piece." The first arrangement choice is whether to follow the opponent's structure or to follow your own.

The second of the two arrangement choices that come up when we attack arguments is, how completely to develop the attack as we present it? What do we include in the presentation of the attack? Let me tell you first what the ideal answer is, according to most of the textbooks on argumentation.

Most of the textbooks say that what you want to do is to present a complete attack. A complete attack includes the following things. First, it includes a statement of the argument that you're going to attack, stated in neutral language—not trying to load the deck—in language that the audience would agree upon, and if it all possible, using the very language that your opponent used in making the argument. Second, what you ought to do is you ought to explain the basis of your attack. What is it that you are going to say about this argument? Third, you develop the attack and support the attack with evidence and explanation. Fourth and finally, having made the attack, you explain the significance of what you've accomplished by making the attack. So you state the argument that's going to be attacked; you state what you're going to do with it; you develop and support the attack; and then you state what's been accomplished by the attack. That's the ideal answer about how to develop the attack.

The problem is that process takes a lot of time, and if done repeatedly, attack after attack, it could get cumbersome, and you could even come off seeming fairly pedantic. The question is, in any given case, how much of that should you do? How fully should you develop the attack? It depends upon how obvious your attack is; how clear it will be to the audience what you're going after in going after a particular argument; and how clear it will be, what you've accomplished once you have done it. These are obviously strategic judgments that need to be made case by case.

Notice that in the Kennedy-Nixon debate example, Kennedy didn't go through all of those four steps when he made each one of his attacks. He didn't restate the argument from the questioner. He only hints at the basis of his attack, and he gives short-hand what has been accomplished by the attack into a very short set of phrases. Why? Because he has limited time, he only has two-and-half minutes; he wants to make several attacks against this argument, and he wants to establish that he's turning around and suggesting that Nixon doesn't state his figures accurately. He needs to do all of that in about two-and half-minutes. So, Kennedy (because I'm sure he didn't sit down and map this out) instinctively made the judgment that in making the attacks, he could eliminate some of those steps in the ideal presentation, and he'd be okay because the audience would be able to follow along. This is the kind of judgment that you need to make whenever you're launching an attack. The two arrangement choices are whether to follow the same organizational structure as the argument you're responding to, and how fully to develop the attack.

We focused between the last lecture and the current one on selection and arrangement choices related to attacking arguments. Now I want to switch over and talk about defending arguments. The first thing we will notice is that the strategic choices available to the defense are much more limited. It's not a good selection choice, for example, to ignore an attack. Once an attack has been made, you want to defend the argument; you pretty much have to respond to the attack. What kinds of selection considerations come into place? How one characterizes the attack might determine how one goes about responding to it.

For instance, you could demonstrate that the attack is inapplicable to the case. Let's suppose that your original argument in your case was that the Social Security Trust Fund will be depleted by the year 2042. The attack in response to that was to say, "Wait a minute, the Social Security Trust Fund is large now and it's been growing since the 1980s, since the last time we reformed Social Security." If your case is that it's going to be depleted in 2042, you could pretty easily point out that this attack is not applicable. Your case is talking about trends that are going to take place in the future, and the attack has dealt with the past; it's simply not applicable.

Another thing you could do is to demonstrate that the attack is trivial in its consequences. Let's go back to the example I used a few lectures ago about mandatory standardized testing of students in school. One of the arguments that was made, that we're doing too much testing, cited the fact that we give the Preliminary Scholastic Assessment Test, the PSAT, in tenth grade. Suppose the attack says, "No, no, no. The PSAT is given in eleventh grade, so we're okay as far as tenth grade is concerned." Remember, the question here is, what are the effects of repeated standardized testing on an overall educational curriculum? Does it really matter whether we give the PSAT in tenth grade or eleventh grade? You could dismiss this attack by saying, "You know, this is of such small consequence that even if it's correct, it really doesn't damage or imperil our position, so we're not going to focus on which grade this test is given." That's another choice.

Or you could demonstrate that the attack is inadequately established. This time we'll imagine a family situation. The original argument is when a teenager makes a case wanting to have the family car out past midnight and the parents respond, "You know, you are always testing limits. Every time we set up a rule you try to get around it." The teenager responds, "That's not so. This is a special case. It's the only time I've made this request." Advice to the teenager: If you want to make this argument, make sure the facts are with you on that one. But what the teenager is trying to do is to defend the original argument by saying the attack is not adequately established, it's faulty; it's based on evidence that's either not there or that is mistaken.

Or you could demonstrate that the attack is simply wrong, that it's in error. The attack says that there's an inconsistency in the way the airlines price for tickets depending on distance that you travel. The defense might say, "No, there's no inconsistency. Most of the pricing structure is pretty reasonable, and where there are discrepancies there are good explanations for them." You could characterize the attack as inapplicable, as trivial, as inadequately established, or as an error. You could probably do other things, too. You could probably say it doesn't outweigh the case, and so on. But the most basic selection choice that you have is not when you respond to the attack; it's how you present the argument in the first place that may determine what attacks can be made against the argument and what cannot.

Before I completely leave selection choices, I want to say another thing about them. When you defend an argument, your defense really has a two-faced nature to it. On the one hand, you're rebuilding your argument; you're rebuilding a position that's been attacked, and that's where your choices are fairly limited. But you're also attacking the attack. When you think about it that way, you have a wider range of choices. We can go back to the last lecture and talk about all the selection choices that are involved in attacks, and they can be applied here. But the danger is that if you think about a defense only as an attack on an attack, you'll lose sight of your original argument, which, after all, you're trying to rebuild. We have to keep both aspects of the defense of arguments in mind.

Still, in all, the selection choices are fairly few, and the arrangement choice in defending an argument is basically whether the structure of the original argument or the structure of the attack will be the dominant organizational plan. Each one of these choices has a pitfall to it. You want to be careful if you choose to make the structure of the original argument your plan; you want to be careful that you don't just repeat the original argument without extending it or responding to the attack.

Let's suppose my original argument was that congestion in major airports creates delays, which lead to economic losses. Suppose your response is to say, "Look, there's not a serious problem of congestion in most of our major airports. It's limited to a small number, and these can be addressed individually. There's not a serious problem." I respond, "But you didn't deny that congested airports create delays that lead to economic losses." I just repeat my argument. Now it's true, you didn't deny that there's a link between congestion and economic losses, but what you did was to deny that there was any serious congestion. You attacked the evidence even though you didn't deny the inference; and so for me to just to repeat the inference will not help me very much at all. That's the pitfall on going back to your own organizational structure.

On the other hand, if you let the structure of the attack govern you, the danger is that the attack will run away with the argument, so that the attack, rather than the argument, becomes the dominant focus.

For instance, let's imagine I've presented a case arguing that stem cell research should be strictly limited. You've provided a lot of different reasons for why limits aren't appropriate and broader support for stem cell research is needed. Suppose I come back and say, "I said that stem cell research should be seriously limited; let's consider all the attacks that were brought against it. The first attack was so and so; well, let me say this about it. The second one was so and so; here's my response to that. The third was this one; here's how I answer that." I lose track of my own position. I've spent all of my time emphasizing your attacks, not my original position in favor of limiting stem cell research. Thus, we want to try to avoid both of these pitfalls, both the pitfall of just repeating and the pitfall of letting the attack run away with the argument. We try for a middle-range position in which the focus is on the original argument, but in which we're also sensitive to the individual attacks, and comment about those.

I said that there wasn't as much to say about defense as about attack. We've covered what the basic selection considerations are and what the basic arrangement considerations are. So let's look at an example. Let's go back to the same example we talked about last time, the Kennedy-Nixon debates of 1960. I want to pick up where I left off then. Remember that the original argument presented by Douglas Kater, the panelist, was that Kennedy's platform would cost $10 billion more than Nixon's, and that Kennedy attacked this argument by re-contextualizing it, providing counter examples, admitting some increases, and challenging the accuracy of Nixon's figures.

Now it's Nixon's turn to rebuild, to defend his original argument. Let's look at the choices that Nixon makes and see how they relate to what we've been discussing. Here is Nixon's response: "Senator Kennedy has indicated on several occasions in this program tonight that I have been misstating his record and his figures. I will issue a white paper after this broadcast quoting exactly what he has said on compulsory arbitration, for example, and the record will show that I have been correct." That's the first part of Nixon's response.

Notice what he did; he picked up on the very last thing that Kennedy said, "You've been misstating your figures." Of course, his honor is being attacked, so he feels the need to defend himself; but he doesn't really talk about the figures on the budget. He talks about another argument in which Kennedy says his position has been misrepresented on compulsory arbitration. That's the very first thing Nixon does to try to defend himself as he responds to this charge of misstating figures, but he doesn't respond to it directly.

Then, Nixon talks about Kennedy's counter-examples and he says the following: "Now as far as his figures are concerned here tonight, he again is engaging in this, what I would call mirror game of 'here it is and here it isn't.'" Look at what Nixon is doing there: he's labeling Kennedy's argument strategy. Remember, we said in the last lecture that labeling the argument strategy is a way to call attention to the strategy and to defeat its effectiveness.

Then, he talks about some of the specific counter-examples, and he tries to suggest that they are illusory, that they're not real counter-examples. On the one hand, for example, he suggests that as far as his medical care program is concerned, that really isn't a problem because it's from Social Security; but Social Security is a tax. The people pay it. It comes right out of their paychecks. This doesn't mean that the people aren't going to be paying the bill. Remember, Kennedy had used Social Security as an example because it's off-budget, so it's not going to add to the cost of his program to the federal budget. Nixon's point is that this is an illusory savings, because people are going to pay the tax.

Nixon goes on to say, "He also indicates that as far as his agricultural program is concerned that he feels that it will cost less than ours. Well, all that I can suggest is that all the experts who have studied the program indicate that it is the most fantastic program, the worst program insofar as its effect on the farmers that America has ever had foisted upon it in an election year or any other time." Nixon's certainly riled up, but you notice he doesn't respond to Kennedy's claim that the agricultural program will cost less. He then introduces a new argument saying that, "Part of the cost of the program that Kennedy left out is a 25 percent rise in food prices that people would have to pay." That's not documented, but what he's suggesting is that there is a hidden cost.

Nixon continues, "Then he goes on to say that he's going to change the interest rate situation and that we're going to get some money that way. Well, what he is saying there, in effect, is that we're going to have inflation. We're going to go right back to what we had under Mr. Truman when he had political control of the Federal Reserve Board. I don't believe we ought to pay our bills through inflation through a phony interest rate." Of course, what Kennedy had been talking about was that by cutting the budget deficit, you'd be able to reduce the interest rates, and what Nixon is saying is that you're going to have inflation and that's not a good thing.

Notice that one of Kennedy's counterexamples, closing loopholes, gets no response from Nixon. Notice that Nixon never draws together what he's accomplished by responding to these counterexamples; they're pretty scattershot responses. He attacks this one for this reason, and this one for this reason, and this one for another reason. Notice also that Nixon doesn't respond to Kennedy's argument that increased spending in certain areas is a good thing; and there's no response at all to the main point that Kennedy had made, which was that he was fiscally responsible and was going to achieve a balanced budget.

If we think about Nixon's response, notice also that he doesn't go back to the original argument, which is that Kennedy's program will cost more than his; nor does he focus on the structure of Kennedy's attacks, suggesting that item by item, the attack falls short. He does a little bit of this and a little bit of that, picking and choosing in ways that probably are strategically not the best for him. Nixon was an accomplished debater—I don't mean to question his ability at all—but in this example, we can see what he's done is made choices about selection and arrangement of his defense that were probably not the best strategic choices.

The reason that we're focusing so systematically in these two lectures on the choices that people can make is so that we can get a sense of them; so that when we're in actual arguments, we will put into practice what we're exploring, and over time, we'll become instinctively more skillful in making the strategic choices that do us the most good.

What we've seen here is the deployment of the defense choices on the part of Nixon in the Kennedy-Nixon debates, and we've seen earlier the deployment of the attack choices on the part of Senator Kennedy. So we've talked about both attack and defense.

Now I want to discuss some general approaches to refutation that can be used in both attack and defense—general strategies that can be used not only attack to an argument but also to rebuild it once it has been attacked. There are a number of these. One of them goes by the Latin term, *Reductio ad absurdum*, "reducing to absurdity." This is a device to suggest that the other arguer's position—whether you're the attacker or the defender—should be rejected because it leads to unacceptable implications. It's not absurd in the sense that you'd laugh at it; it's absurd in the sense that it leads to a result that nobody would accept.

For instance, you say, "Catsup is a vegetable," and some people did during the 1980s. If catsup is a vegetable, then salt and pepper are carbohydrates, relish is a fruit, mustard is a protein, and we can have a balanced diet consisting of nothing but condiments. This is an obviously unacceptable result, and because what leads us to that unacceptable result is the standard that says catsup is a vegetable, we reject that position. That's *Reductio ad absurdum*.

Another one of these general devices of refutation is called turning the tables. This means showing how a position that is claimed by one arguer actually benefits the other arguer. Let's talk about airline safety one more time. Let's imagine that you are making an argument. You want to improve airline safety and you say the way to do that is to build more airports in order to reduce congestion at the existing major airports. Let's imagine that I'm responding to you and I say, "You want to improve airline safety. What will really improve airline safety is not to build more airports, which will just boost demand. What will really improve airline safety is more careful scheduling controls, improved safety procedures for the airlines' taking off and landing; in other words, more regulation, not more freedom." If safety is the goal, safety doesn't work to you advantage as a reason to build more airports; it works to my advantage as a reason to increase regulation. I've turned the tables on you. I've taken your value and used it for my purposes.

Another general means of refutation is to pose a dilemma, to suggest that the opposing arguer must choose between unattractive alternatives. A critic of the George W. Bush administration might say, "You want to overcome the economic slump and to improve the rate of job creation. There are only two ways to do that. We have to reduce the federal budget deficit either by reducing the expense on the war in Iraq or by increasing taxes. You don't want to do either one, but those are the only two things that are going to make enough difference to the budget to get us out of the economic slump and pick up the pace of job creation." The dilemma poses unattractive alternatives and suggests that those are the only alternatives. And so, if you're right, that they are the only alternatives, the dilemma can be a very potent means of refutation.

Another one—in addition to *Reductio ad absurdum,* turning the tables, posing dilemmas—is the argument from residues, which dictates what position your opponent can be in by eliminating all of the other possibilities. This was a favorite form of argument by President Lyndon Johnson during the Vietnam War when he would defend his position against his critics by saying, "Look, we have only three alternatives; we can turn tail and run," which is the way he characterized withdrawal, not exactly in neutral language, "we can pour it on, bomb them back to the Stone Age, and risk World War

III; or we can persevere in the course that we're in." What he's doing is he's responding to attack by saying there's only this one choice.

Then there's the argument *a fortiori*. This is an argument of comparison that suggests that what's true of the lesser is true of the greater, or vice versa. If it's important to count the votes accurately in an uncontested race, all the more should we count them accurately in a closely contested race.

A final general means of refutation—I've suggested this before—is to identify contradictions or inconsistencies in the opponent's argument that will eliminate at least one of the other arguer's positions as well as questioning the other arguer's general credibility.

These, then, are approaches that are available to both attack and defense. The processes of attack and defense together help to move the argument forward by identifying and focusing on what is in dispute. So, as we've said, they are constructive and very important processes. Next time we'll talk about another aspect of putting arguments together, and that's the language and style in which they're cast.

Lecture Eleven
Language and Style in Argument

Scope:

This lecture completes a series that addresses the development of arguments into cases and the dynamics of controversy created by the presentation of a case. Here, the specific concern is with choices related to language and presentational style. Everyday arguments are embedded in language, and language is not a neutral instrument for conveying content. Neither is it adornment that is added on to an argument's "real" content. Rather, language is itself a factor in the argument, and how an argument is presented is part of its content. This lecture will explore how definitions, figurative language, precision, and intensity contribute to argumentation and how they affect the presentation of a case.

Outline

I. Language is a resource in everyday argumentation.

    A. Arguments are cast in language and are not reducible to the formulas of formal logic.

    B. Language is an intrinsic aspect of the argument, not something that is added for ornamentation.

    C. Arguers make choices about language, which serves as a strategic resource.

II. Definitions are a strategic resource for the arguer.

    A. Definitions serve many purposes.

        1. They characterize common usage.

        2. They make vague terms more precise.

        3. They invent new usage.

    B. Of special interest to argumentation is the persuasive definition.

        1. This is a form of slanting in which a definition is used to gain an argumentative advantage.

        2. Such a definition alters the meaning of a term by associating it with a term of clear positive or negative connotation.

    3. It transfers emotional meaning from one denotation to another.

    4. There are many contemporary examples, such as the "death tax" for the estate tax, the "nuclear option" for a Senate rules change to limit filibusters, and "partial-birth abortion" for a specific medical procedure.

  C. Definitions are used in argumentation to alter the scope of the conflict.

    1. The would-be loser may redefine the conflict to enlist the effort of others who previously have not been involved.

    2. Sometimes, conversely, definitions may be used to restrict the scope of the argument by excluding otherwise interested parties.

III. Definitions should be clear enough to avoid common fallacies of meaning.

  A. Equivocation is the use of the same word to convey different meanings in the same argument.

  B. Ambiguity results when we cannot be sure which of a set of possible meanings of a term is the intended meaning.

  C. Amphiboly results when we cannot be sure which of a set of possible meanings of a phrase is the intended meaning.

  D. Vagueness is a situation in which a term or concept is indeterminate as to meaning.

  E. Heaps and slippery slopes are patterns in which boundaries or dividing lines, being imprecise, are treated as if they were nonexistent.

  F. These errors come about from the inexactness of language, a condition peculiar to informal argument.

IV. Linguistic precision, however, can have argumentative implications.

  A. Imprecise language is not always undesirable.

    1. It may leave options open for later consideration.

    2. It may allow parties with divergent interests to agree on a goal but to do so for different reasons.

  B. Strategies are available to make language less precise.

    1. Euphemisms can serve this purpose.

2. Ambiguity, equivocation, and vagueness—previously identified as fallacies—can be used intentionally to achieve this purpose.

C. Strategies are available to make language more precise.
   1. Stipulative or operational definitions can serve this purpose.
   2. Drawing analogies to other arguments can serve this purpose.
   3. Naming the argument can serve this purpose.

V. Figures of speech, rather than being merely ornamentation, also have argumentative implications.
   A. They may increase the presence of a concept.
      1. This involves making it more salient, bringing it to the foreground of consciousness.
      2. Presence makes the abstract concrete and evokes realities that are distant in time and space.
      3. Analogy, metaphor, and simile all function to increase presence.
      4. Other approaches to increasing presence include repetition, accumulation of details, and accent.

   B. They may suggest a choice among alternatives.
      1. The use of antithesis obviously poses a choice.
      2. Metaphors suggesting persuasive definition can be used to pose choices.

   C. They may increase communion with the audience through references to common activities or experiences.

   D. Abraham Lincoln's "House Divided" speech illustrates the argumentative significance of figures of speech.
      1. He uses the metaphor "machinery" to refer to the means used in an imagined plot to make slavery national.
      2. He uses the metaphor of industrial "bosses" to refer to the plotters.
      3. He uses the metaphor of building a frame house to refer to the unfolding of the plot.
      4. He uses accumulation of historical details to suggest the success of the plot so far.

5. He uses repetition of the phrase "plainly enough now" to create a sense of revelation of what previously had been hidden.

VI. From these examples, we can conclude that language and methods of composition and persuasion are not neutral.

    A. They are part of the substance of an argument, not separate from it.

    B. They affect the strategic positions and interest of the arguers.

    C. They affect the context and perspective within which arguments will be perceived.

Essential Reading:

James A. Herrick, *Argumentation: Understanding and Shaping Arguments*, pp. 157–172.

"Figures of Speech," in Thomas O. Sloane, ed., *Encyclopedia of Rhetoric*, pp. 309–314.

Supplementary Reading:

Charles L. Stevenson, *Ethics and Language*, chapter 8.

Douglas Walton, "Persuasive Definitions and Public Policy Arguments," *Argumentation and Advocacy* 37 (Winter 2001), pp. 117–132.

Richard D. Rieke and Malcolm O. Sillars, *Argumentation and Critical Decision Making*, pp. 291–305.

Questions to Consider:

1. Persuasive definition has been referred to as an argumentative strategy. Can it also be a means to prevent argument by substituting a definition for a case? How can this danger be minimized?

2. What are the similarities and differences between figures of speech and deductive argument forms with respect to enhancing presence and awareness of thoughts and ideas?

Lecture Eleven—Transcript
Language and Style in Argument

For the past several lectures we've been talking about aspects of argumentation strategy and tactics—being able to recognize and diagram both simple and complex arguments, case construction, stasis, attack and defense of arguments. There's one more major topic that I want to take up under this general heading, and that's the way that language and style work in argumentation.

This lecture is really built around a fairly obvious claim that has implications that are not quite so obvious, and that is that arguments are cast in language. The sorts of arguments that we have every day are not reducible to the symbols of mathematics or formal logic—all A is B, all B is C, if P then Q, and so on. The language in which our arguments are cast is not simply a dressing or covering that we put on to the substance of the argument itself. It's very much bound up with the argument itself, and the way in which arguments are cast in language has some profound effects for understanding the nature of the argument.

What's more, arguers make choices about language, just as they make choices about case construction and attack and defense. These choices serve as a strategic resource. As with other choices, they often make them unthinkingly, but we want to be systematic in our ability to understand and talk about them. Recognizing that we can't separate substance and language, or substance and style, that they're bound up together, let's look if we can at some of the ways in which language and style figure into argumentation.

Let me begin with definitions. "Now there's a dry subject," you might think. And yet, definitions are a really important strategic resource for an arguer. Let's remind ourselves, first of all, of the different purposes that definitions serve. The most obvious one is to characterize common usage, to talk about how people ordinarily use a term, what they mean by it. Those are the definitions that we find in a dictionary. Sometimes, definitions are used to make vague terms more precise. You may have noticed that in these lectures there have been a number of technical terms, I hope not too many, but that when I've introduced technical terms, I've done so in order to give us a precise meaning, a clear meaning, or clear understanding for a concept that might otherwise be vague.

Definitions are also used to invent or to characterize new usage. In the past 10 or 15 years, we've seen loads of examples of this related to information technology. Terms like "boot up," "surf the net," "download," and "Google" as a verb, for example, are all terms that characterize usage that didn't exist prior to the personal computer age. Those are all purposes that definitions serve.

There's another purpose that is particularly important for the use of definitions in argumentation, and that is the persuasive definition, or a definition that conceals an argument within it. It's almost an invitation to have an argument. This is a form in which definitions are used to gain an argumentative advantage for one person or another. They alter the meaning of a term by associating that term with either positively valued terms or negatively valued terms, in the hope that the positive or negative value will transfer from the other terms to the one for which we use the persuasive definition. That's the theory—persuasive definition transfers emotional meaning from one term to another.

Let's try to understand this theory a little bit more with a simple example. As a college professor, one of the things that I occasionally encounter is to receive from a student a paper that has been found to be copied from another student, or from a printed source, or, increasingly, from the Internet. It's been plagiarized. What do I call the act that has taken place? Do I call it carelessness or sloppiness? These are terms that would suggest unintentional error, calling for a classic teachable moment in which I explain to the student how to be more careful, how to make sure that he or she uses sources that are his or her own. It would seem to be certainly a mistake, but with nothing malicious about it, nothing intended to deceive.

But what if I call it fraud or theft of another person's ideas? Now I've put it in an entirely different context. I've suggested intent, and motive, and maliciousness. In one case, I've defined this act as carelessness, and in another case I've defined the act as fraud. The definitions are persuasive because there are connotations bound up in those terms, like "carelessness" or "fraud." Obviously, it makes a difference in how I'm going to respond to this behavior, based on what I think of the act and how I'm going to evaluate the student who was involved in it. In other words, these are not neutral or trivial choices of language, to define the act one way or another.

When we do this in an argument, our definitions affect the perception of the argument and of how to respond to the argument. There are many contemporary examples of just this kind of a use of persuasive definition. For example, the estate tax has been referred to by its opponents as the "death tax." The connotations that are involved in calling it the "death tax" are pretty obvious. The suggestion that death should somehow be a taxable event, as if the tax were on the person who died rather than on the person who inherits this windfall estate, makes the tax objectionable and helps the cause for elimination of the task.

In another example, the Democrats in the Senate who were concerned that the rules might be changed to eliminate filibusters on judicial candidates referred to this rule change as the "nuclear option." Of course, the connotation of "nuclear option" is that this would be a devastating blow to the civility and the procedures of the Senate, almost like dropping a nuclear bomb. This would not be a minor change or a different way in counting up the votes.

Or, citing a particularly obvious example in the early years of the 21st century, a particular medical procedure that has the name "intact dilation and extraction" has been called, by its opponents, "partial-birth abortion." Of course, calling this procedure "partial-birth abortion" is not neutral at all. It's a way to mobilize objection to this particular procedure by suggesting that it is especially gruesome and inhumane. Notice, in all of these examples, the argument is cast in a particular language. The language is an attempt to define some key terms, but the definition is not neutral. The definition affects the way in which the argument is perceived and is dealt with.

How are definitions used? One of the ways that they are used in arguments is to widen or narrow the scope of the conflict—to widen or narrow what the dispute is about, and consequently, who might be in a position to have something to say about the dispute. It happens in two ways. First, definitions can be used to widen the scope of argument. The person who stands to lose the argument if it's confined to a narrow scope may seek to widen the scope.

For example, what happens if we refer to budget deficits as immoral? Once we enlarge the scope of the argument to refer not just to technical economics but to morality, we have broadened the circle of people who have something legitimate to say about the argument.

It's not just economists. It's not just a professional dispute. It's not just a technical matter. It's a matter that raises questions of principles and morals about which anybody is qualified to be involved or to have something to say. If you stand to lose by having the argument be construed narrowly, you define it in such a way as to broaden the scope.

It can also work the other way around. Definitions can be used to restrict the scope of argument by excluding otherwise interested parties. There's a famous speech in which President Kennedy said that, "The management of a modern economy is increasingly technical in nature." This is an attempt to do the opposite of my first example. To say, if it is technical in nature, then the people who are qualified to say something about it are those with technical expertise and training, not ordinary citizens.

Or, when in discussing missile defense some advocate said, "The concept of throw weight and how it's measured is an increasingly technical kind of problem." It's to suggest that people who don't have this kind of technical training should stay out of the argument because they're not qualified to say anything about it. Definitions can be used to alter not only the connotations of a term, but the scope of the dispute of the controversy itself.

However they're used, as a general rule definitions ought to be clear enough that they avoid some common errors in meaning. I want to talk briefly about some of those errors, and it will be pretty obvious why they're things we generally tried to avoid. One of them is equivocation. Equivocation is the use of a term in two different senses in the same argument, so that the meaning subtly changes, and, if we're not careful, one can lose track of the original argument.

For example, look at the parent who says to a teenager, "I trust you. I have always trusted you, and therefore I trust you will be home by midnight." The term trust means something different in that last statement. It means, "I expect you to be home by midnight." It's not referring to trusting one's judgment or placing one's trust in another person, as it is in the beginning of an argument.

My favorite example of equivocation, by the way, is an argument that's set up almost like a syllogism. It goes, "I love you, therefore I am a lover. All the world loves a lover. You are all the world to me, therefore you love me." You might want to try this and see if it has any benefit for you, but it should be pretty obvious that several of the terms change meaning during the course of the argument: what love means, what a lover is, what all the world is, and so on. That's equivocation.

The second thing we want to avoid as we use definitions is ambiguity. Most of the time, we want to avoid ambiguity. It's a situation in which a word has multiple meanings and we can't tell from the argument which meaning is intended. Take the simple statement, "The cardinals are in town." Do we mean birds? Do we mean a baseball team? Or do we mean officials of the Roman Catholic Church? We can't tell simply from the statement. It's ambiguous.

A close cousin of ambiguity is amphiboly. This is a lesser-known term, but what it refers to a phrase—not a single word, but a phrase—that has multiple meanings, and you can't tell just from the statement which one is intended. My favorite example of this is something that I always threaten to do, but honestly, I've never actually done it. I'm asked often to write letters of recommendation for students, and though some of those I'm very happy to do, some are much more difficult to write. I've thought about writing a letter of recommendation that says, "I can't recommend this student highly enough. No one would be better for the position that you advertise." Think about it. Does that statement mean there are no superlatives that I could use that would capture the student; or does it mean the student is not very good, that I can't recommend him enough to be supporting him positively? You can't tell simply from the statement itself. That's amphibole.

We have equivocation, ambiguity, amphibole; vagueness is another problem with definitions. Vagueness is a situation in which a term or concept is indeterminate as to what it means; there's no way to pin it down. I'm sometimes asked how old someone is and I used to say, "Well, he's middle-aged." What does middle-aged mean? At one point in my life I thought it was anybody over 25; and then as I've aged, my understanding of middle-aged has changed proportionately. I now think 85 and up is a pretty good definition of middle-age. The point is, there's no way to pin it down. It's an inherently vague term; and as a general rule we want to try to avoid vagueness.

Then there is a pair of problems that are related. They're the mirror image of each other, and they go by the names "the heap" and "the slippery slope." They both involve using language that refers to making distinctions that are hard to make precisely, and so suggests that they can't be made at all.

For example, let's talk about "the heap." If you're watching this on video, you can tell the color of my beard. If you're stuck with the audio version, I'll tell you that it's gray or white, depending on your point of view. Thirty-five years ago when I grew it, it was very dark. At some point there was gray hair, but that didn't change the overall color of my beard; we still referred to it as dark. Then there was another gray hair. One more hair didn't make a difference; another one didn't make a difference. No one hair made any difference in the color of my beard; therefore, how could the color has changed? That's the heap. Because we can't identify the point of change, we say there's no change. This, by the way, was an argument strategy that was used during the Vietnam War. With each escalation in the number of troops, there were official pronouncements that this was not a widening of the war or a change in our basic mission, but somehow, as we got from 16,000 to 500,000 troops, it became an American war. That's the heap.

The slippery slope is just the opposite. It's setting off a chain of events that you assume can't ever be stopped—a chain of consequences. I have students who come to me and say, "Please let me into your class, because if I can't get into your class, I can't fulfill the requirements; and then I can't have this major; and if I don't have this major I can't graduate; and if I can't graduate, I'll have to turn down this job that's been to offered to me; and if I turn down this job, I'm going to seriously weaken my long term income possibilities; and if I weaken my income possibilities, it will hurt my mental health; and if I hurt my mental health, I'm going to be more likely to be suicidal. So, let me into your course or I will commit suicide." Now that's a slippery slope. It's a set of events that is alleged to be unstoppable, and it leads to a result that is far fetched from the point at which it starts off.

This was also widely used in official U.S. government rhetoric during much of the Cold war under the heading of "The Domino Theory." One of the sections I didn't talk about from the Kennedy-Nixon Debates involved the islands of Quemoy and Matsu, off the coast of mainland China. The argument was that if they fell to the Communists, Formosa would be next; and if Formosa fell, then Japan; if Japan, then the Philippines; if the Philippines, then Thailand; if Thailand, then Malaya; and all of the sudden, from the loss of these islands that were the size of postage stamps, we would have Communism surging across the Pacific Ocean and threatening all of the world. That's the slippery slope.

All of these errors—equivocation, ambiguity, amphibole, vagueness, heaps, slippery slopes—come about from the inexactness of language, which is a condition that's particular to informal argument. Language is messy. You might think, therefore, that what we ought to do is to make our language at least as precise as we can. That's a good general rule, but not always. Sometimes imprecise language is desirable. Why is it that diplomatic statements are often rendered in ambiguous language? To leave options open for later consideration. Why else might things be rendered ambiguously or imprecisely? To allow parties with different interests to agree on something, even though they have different reasons and different points of view.

For example, the Congress of the United States passed a resolution apologizing for slavery prior to the Civil War. The apology was fairly vague because some people believed that they were personally responsible, and some didn't. Some believed that reparations should be paid, and some didn't. Some believed that slavery was a continuing blight on our landscape; some believed that we should get over. But they could come together around fairly general language to express this statement of apology.

Sometimes we want language to be less precise. When that happens, there are ways to do it. One is the euphemism, a term that cloaks meaning in a fairly general kind of statement. If you study the history of the American Civil War, you'll know that in the years immediately after the war, different terms were used to refer to it. Sometimes it was called the War of Southern Rebellion; or conversely, the War of Northern Aggression, by people who wanted to rub raw the wounds. For people who wanted to heal, it was sometimes called the War Between the States; or my favorite, The Late Unpleasantness. That's an imprecise term if ever there was one, and it's deliberately chosen in order to not reopen the controversy.

Ambiguity, equivocation, vagueness—the very things I just talked about as errors sometimes can be used deliberately to make language less precise. For example, in the 1970s when President Richard Nixon went to China, there was a communiqué that was issued in Shanghai that said, "Everybody agrees that there is but one China, and Taiwan is part of China" This statement was seemingly clear and yet ambiguous. Did that mean mainland China would eventually encompass Taiwan? Or that the nationalist China in Taiwan would eventually re-conquer mainland China? It was deliberately an unanswered question.

On the other hand, most of the time we want to make language more precise, and we can do that sometimes by stipulative definitions. For example, take a parent and child who disagree on what it means for the child to clean up his room. The parent says, "Now by a clean room, I mean no clothes on the floor, all the things put away on the shelves, and so on." You stipulate the operations to be performed and you thereby make the definition more precise.

Drawing analogies to other arguments can make language more precise. If we want to understand gender discrimination we say, "This is just like racial discrimination," which we presumably understand more clearly. Or we name or label the argument. President George W. Bush referred to "the vision thing." Sometimes people who wanted to criticize him talked about "the vision thing argument" referring to general goals or objectives.

We have definitions and we have precise or imprecise language. Figures of speech, which we think of if we studied them in English class as ornamentation, also have argumentative implications. They affect the way an argument is perceived. For example, consider some metaphors; during much of the Cold war, Communism was talked about as a cancer. If we understand communism as cancer, it tells us what we ought to do: we ought to detect it early and remove it early before it gets be to fatal. The war in Iraq has sometimes been discussed by its critics as a quagmire, and the metaphor of quagmire suggests we're sinking deeper and deeper in, and it's going to be hard if not impossible to extricate ourselves. In the last 30 years, all manner of political scandals have been referred to with the suffix -*gate*, which, of course, conjures up the image of Watergate, and suggests an analogy—here is a comparison of scandals. Just a couple of lectures ago I said, "Think about how the military metaphor can mislead us when we talk about attack and defense of arguments."

Figures of speech make a concept more salient; they bring it to the forefront of our consciousness. Other figures of speech suggest a choice, as for example, antithesis: when President Kennedy talked about "Not a pledge but a request. I offer you not luxury, but sacrifice." Metaphors can also be used to pose choices, like the cancer metaphor: are we going to cut it out, or are we going to let it grow until it kills us? Figures of speech also can increase a sense of communion between the arguer and the audience through references to common activities or experiences. For example, the quagmire metaphor in the case of Iraq for most people over a certain age evokes memories of Vietnam, for which the term "quagmire" was so often used.

Just like definitions and precise language, figures of speech have argumentative implications. There's a very famous speech that illustrates a number of these ideas; it's a speech delivered by Abraham Lincoln when he accepted the nomination to run for the U.S. Senate against Stephen A. Douglas. It's the *House Divided* speech, in which Lincoln said, "A house divided against itself cannot stand." We often misunderstand this speech. Lincoln was not predicting the Civil War; what he was predicting was that the country would become all free or all slave, and that it was moving in the direction of being all slave. Most people would think this a preposterous idea, the evidence for it was flimsy; but Lincoln effectively used language and style to support that argument.

For instance, he uses the metaphor of machinery to refer to an alleged plan to make slavery national. He says, "Let anyone who doubts carefully contemplate that now almost complete legal combination, piece of machinery, so to speak, compounded of the Nebraska Doctrine and the Dred Scott Decision." To suggest that this is deliberate, he refers to the designers of this plan as "its chief architects" and the executers of this plan as "its chief bosses."

Lincoln criticizes Stephen A. Douglas' position, popular sovereignty, which he talks about as scaffolding. He says, "Under the Dred Scott Decision, squatter sovereignty squatted out of existence, tumbled down like temporary scaffolding, like the mold at the foundry, served through one blast and fell back into loose sand."

He uses the metaphor of building a house to refer to the unfolding of the plot. He can't prove the plot directly, so he argues it by metaphor. "When we see a lot of framed timbers," he said, "different portions of which we know have been gotten out at different times and places and by different workmen...and we see these timbers joined together, and see they exactly make the frame of a house or a mill...or if a single piece be lacking, we see the place in the frame exactly fitted and prepared, yet to bring such a piece in, in such a case we find it impossible not to believe that Stephen, and Franklin, and Roger, and James all understood one another from the beginning, and all worked upon a common plan or draft drawn up before the first blow was struck."

How does he prove there's a plot? He tells a story by metaphor and says, when you see these things happening it's impossible not to believe it; and the metaphor suggests these things are happening. He uses an accumulation of historical details to suggest the success of the plot so far; and he uses a metaphor to refer to Douglas to forestall people from defecting and voting for Douglas. He says, "A living dog is better than a dead lion. Judge Douglas, if not a dead lion for this work, is a caged and toothless one," meaning, you can't rely on Douglas if your goal is to stop to the tendency towards nationwide slavery.

Now, I've covered this speech very briefly, but I hope you can see from these few examples how language becomes a resource in the argument, how it helps Lincoln to develop the position that he is trying to make. Language and style are part of the substance of the argument; they are not separate from it. They affect the strategic positions and the interests of the arguers. Thus, our consideration of argument strategy and tactics needs to include a focus on language and style as well. Next time, we'll start something new.

Lecture Twelve
Evaluating Evidence

Scope:

With this lecture we turn our attention from argument analysis to argument appraisal, and we will focus now on individual arguments rather than overall structures of a case. We begin with the evidence undergirding an argument. It must be agreed to by the arguers for a meaningful discussion to proceed. Evidence can be categorized in various ways, but we will focus on examples, statistics, tangible objects, testimony, and social consensus. Although this lecture discusses normative standards for evidence, in actual arguments the participants sometimes settle for less.

Outline

I. Evidence represents the grounds for a claim.

    A. Several controversies illustrate the significance of evidence in the evaluation of an argument.

        1. In the fall of 2004, *CBS News* was forced to retract a story about President Bush's National Guard service because of faulty evidence.

        2. In the spring of 2005, *Newsweek* magazine retracted a story about mistreatment of Muslim detainees at Guantanamo because of insufficient evidence.

        3. In the 2000 election campaign, television networks twice called the Florida election results prematurely because of misleading evidence.

    B. Evidence answers the question "How do you know?" or "What do you have to go on?" in making a claim.

    C. The evidence should be agreed upon by all participants.

        1. It thereby serves as a secure starting point for the dispute.

        2. If it is contested, discussion of the claim stops until the adequacy of the evidence is established—as the above claims illustrate.

        3. Settling the matter now requires a separate argument in which the original evidence functions as a claim.

D. We must understand what is required to agree on the evidence.

    1. Sometimes there are technical rules, as in law.

    2. In ordinary usage, the test is what a critical audience would accept.

E. Speech-act philosophy provides an operational definition of "providing evidence."

    1. A speaker wants a hearer, who does not accept a claim, to do so willingly and freely.

    2. Both speaker and hearer realize that there are truth conditions for this claim—things that, if they could be established, would show the claim to be true.

    3. The speaker believes that some other statement, not obvious to the hearer, is such a truth condition.

    4. The speaker utters this other statement.

    5. The hearer accepts it, regards it as a truth condition for the claim, and therefore accepts the claim.

II. Abraham Lincoln's Cooper Union address illustrates many different types of evidence.

A. In this 1860 address, Lincoln responds to Stephen Douglas's claim that the Founding Fathers supported his position on the issue of slavery.

B. Lincoln accepted Douglas's premise, but then produced evidence that the Founding Fathers were actually consistent with his position, rather than that of Douglas.

    1. Lincoln relies on historical documents, a kind of tangible object.

    2. He uses shared historical understanding, a kind of social consensus.

    3. He relies on the credibility of the "founding fathers," as stipulated by Stephen Douglas.

    4. He accumulates examples of specific founders and their views.

    5. He refers to congressional organization of the Southwest Territory, where Congress did not prohibit slavery, but did regulate it.

    6. He talks about the prohibition on importing slaves into Louisiana Territory.

    7. He refers to the Missouri Compromise.

C. All of these arguments illustrate congressional regulation of slavery, which Douglas claimed the Founding Fathers opposed. Thus, Lincoln concluded that the majority of the signers of the Constitution believed that Congress had the power to regulate slavery—a position opposed to Douglas's use of the Founding Fathers.

III. Common types of evidence can be grouped under the headings of examples, statistics, tangible objects, testimony, and social consensus.

IV. Examples are one common type of evidence.

    A. Brief mention of an instance, without any development, is one kind of example.

    B. Illustrations are fully developed instances.

    C. Generalizations from the examples may be either stated or implied.

    D. Although one can argue about whether the examples support the generalization, the truth of the examples themselves must be accepted before the argumentation can proceed.

V. Statistics are another form of evidence.

    A. Raw numbers are the simplest statistics.

    B. Percentages, ratios, and index numbers are other statistics.

    C. Measures of central tendency include the mean, the median, and the mode.

    D. Rates of change are statistical measures.

    E. Probability statements (including the outcomes of controlled studies and experiments) are yet another form of statistics.

    F. Each of these statistical forms is subject to tests of its accuracy, because the truth of statistics must be accepted for them to function as evidence in arguments.

VI. Tangible objects are another form of evidence.

    A. These objects figure prominently in criminal law, as in the importance of finding the murder weapon, for instance.

    B. Sometimes they are important historically, as in the discovery of ancient artifacts.

C. The significance of tangible objects is captured in the adage that a picture is worth a thousand words.

D. Sometimes, though, words will be tangible objects—as in the example of a historical document.

VII. Testimony of fact or opinion is another kind of evidence.

    A. We rely on testimony about things that we cannot know directly or about which we are not qualified to have a reliable opinion.

    B. The testimony is accepted because of the credibility of the source.

        1. The classical concept of *ethos* is the basis of credibility.

        2. Credibility is a function of competence (expertise), trustworthiness, good will, and dynamism.

    C. Credibility can be established for oneself or derived from the use of other credible sources.

        1. Eyewitness access to information will make one a credible source.

        2. Background and training will make one a credible source.

        3. A good track record will make one a credible source.

    D. Several factors can place credibility in doubt and require a separate argument to establish the evidence.

        1. Is the person an authority on this subject?

        2. Is there a clear basis on which the person reached the conclusion?

        3. Does the person have a bias or vested interest?

        4. Do credible sources disagree?

VIII. Social consensus consists of beliefs that function as if they were facts.

    A. "Common knowledge" is a type of social consensus.

    B. Shared value judgments are a type of social consensus.

    C. Shared historical understandings are a type of social consensus.

    D. Previously established conclusions are a type of social consensus.

    E. Stipulations in a specific discussion are a type of social consensus.

F. Differences in core values or common knowledge will need to be resolved before social consensus can be accepted as evidence.

IX. Although our concerns are normative, we should note that actual audiences often have looser standards for evidence.

   A. Judgments of quality of the evidence are affected by agreement or disagreement with the claim.

   B. Judgments of quality of the evidence are affected by a speaker's delivery.

   C. Judgments of quality of the evidence are affected by unfamiliarity with the source and our opinion of the person who is using the evidence.

   D. Evidence is most influential when an audience is unfamiliar with the material and when the goal is sustained attitude change over time.

Essential Reading:

James A. Herrick, *Argumentation: Understanding and Shaping Arguments*, pp. 101–148.

"Social Knowledge," in Thomas O. Sloane, ed., *Encyclopedia of Rhetoric*, pp. 721–724.

Supplementary Reading:

Austin J. Freeley and David L. Steinberg, *Argumentation and Debate: Critical Thinking for Reasoned Decision Marking*, chapters 6–7.

Robert P. Newman and Dale R. Newman, *Evidence*.

Richard D. Rieke and Malcolm O. Sillars, *Argumentation and Critical Decision Making*, pp. 123–143, 187–202.

David Zarefsky, *Public Speaking: Strategies for Success*, pp. 123–147.

Questions to Consider:

1. When would each of the categories mentioned in the lecture—examples, statistics, tangible objects, testimony, and social consensus—serve as the best type of evidence?

2. If audiences have looser standards for evidence than those discussed in this lecture, what role should normative standards of evidence play in actual controversies?

Lecture Twelve—Transcript
Evaluating Evidence

For the last several lectures, our focus has been on argumentation strategies and tactics. We've been looking at how we take individual arguments and put them together into larger units. We've looked at the structure of a case, and we've talked about attack and defense. At the end of the last lecture, I promised you that we would now be shifting our focus and taking up something new. And we will. Now, for the next several lectures, I want us to focus on the individual argument as our unit of analyses. This is a kind of switch, if you will, from the macro to the micro level of analysis. We'll talk about the parts of individual arguments, and how we determine if they're strong or if they're weak. We'll be focusing on both argument construction and argument appraisal.

We've already got a head start because, if you remember the different parts of the argument, one of them is the claim. We've talked already about the claim. We did so several lectures ago, when we talked about types of claims, how claims get put together, and how the major claim is called the resolution. We'll count that as done and focus in this lecture on another one of the parts of the argument, which is the evidence, the building block from which the claim is based.

To illustrate that oftentimes what arguments depend upon is the nature of the evidence, let me just briefly remind us of some significant controversies that took place in the early 2000s. In the fall of 2004, CBS news aired a story about President Bush's National Guard service and the allegation that he had been absent from duty. CBS was forced to retract this story because the story was found to be based on faulty evidence. In the spring of 2005, *Newsweek* magazine published a story, which it then had to retract, about the mistreatment of Muslim detainees at Guantanamo Bay in Cuba, particularly the allegation that the Koran had been mistreated or abused. In the 2000 election campaign, networks twice prematurely called the state of Florida, once for Gore and once for Bush, in both cases before the results were conclusive. That led to congressional investigations and changes in the way networks report election results. In every one of those controversies, the outcome of the controversy was based upon the quality of the evidence. In some cases, the claims were never directly denied, but because the evidence was unacceptable, the argument could not proceed. So it's very important that we focus our attention on evidence, and that we understand what's required for evidence to be approved.

Evidence, of course, is what answers the question, "How do you know?" or "What do you have to go on?" when a person makes a claim and the claim is then called into question. Just to remind ourselves of something we've already said, the evidence needs to be agreed to by all of the participants, so that it's a secure starting point for the dispute. If it's contested, discussion of the claim stops until the adequacy of the evidence is established, as the examples I've just cited illustrate. In each case, the controversy about the claim didn't proceed any further because acceptable evidence that people would agree upon could not be marshaled. Settling the matter when evidence is in dispute requires a separate argument in which the original evidence now functions as the claim to be established.

When we say that audiences accept the evidence as to its truth, what's required to do that? Sometimes, as in technical fields, like the law, there are specific rules. That is, for something to count as evidence in a court of law, it must meet certain tests. If it meets the test, we accept it as evidence; if not, we exclude it. For example, what a witness has directly observed can be considered evidence; but what a witness has heard but not observed directly is not considered evidence, it's hearsay, and is ordinarily ruled to be inadmissible. There are some technical rules in particular fields.

However, in ordinary usage, in ordinary argument, the test is, what would a critical audience be likely to accept as true? When I phrase the test that way, notice what I'm saying. An argument's delivered for a particular audience, and we may know lots of things about that specific audience, but that's not enough. It may be that a particular audience will be swayed by astrology, or it might be inclined to accept unsubstantiated claims of conspiracies and plots; but ordinarily a critical audience would not.

To set our standard for acceptability of evidence we must ask, what would a critical audience—an audience that's reasoning and thinking critically—be likely to accept? By the way, speech-act philosophers have worked on this and have come up with a very specific definition of what it means for an audience to accept evidence. You may be interested in this if only for its specificity.

Listen to the following. Providing evidence means: one, a speaker wants a hearer who does not accept a claim to do so, willing and freely. Two, both speaker and hearer realize that there are truth conditions for this claim, There are things that, if they could be established, would show the claim to be true. Three, the speaker believes that some other statement not obvious to the hearer is such a truth condition. Four, the speaker utters this other statement. Five, the hearer accepts it, regards it as a truth condition for the claim, and therefore, accepts the claim.

Now, you may conclude that what that establishes is that speech-act philosophers are pretty pedantic and focus on the obvious. Maybe so, but what they've done is to spell out the following question: What does it mean for us to say that the evidence has got to be provided and acceptable in order for the argument to go further?

Let's explore this in a historical example. Because I talked in the last lecture about Abraham Lincoln, I wanted to use another famous speech of Lincoln's that is built very carefully on evidence. That's the speech that Lincoln gave at Cooper Union in New York in the spring of 1860. He claimed, after the fact, that it was this speech that made him president, and it's certainly a very important speech. What Lincoln does in this speech is to respond to a statement made by Stephen Douglas, that the founding fathers understood the question of slavery in the territories even better than we do know. What Douglas did was to enlist popular reverence for the founding fathers, and to claim that the founding fathers really supported his position on the issue.

What does Lincoln do in the Cooper Union speech? He accepts Douglas's premise that the founding fathers understood the question better than we do, and that was a wise thing for him to do, because everybody revered the founding fathers; but then he proceeded to produce evidence that the founding fathers were actually consistent with his position, not with Douglas'. As I think I mentioned before, this was kind of hard to do on either side, because the founding fathers didn't take any position on the question immediately at hand; one had to infer it.

What does Lincoln do in this speech? He defines the founding fathers as designers of the Constitution and he relies on various forms of evidence. He uses historical documents, which are a kind of tangible object. He uses shared historical understanding, a kind of social consensus. He uses the credibility of the founders that Douglas stipulated. He accumulates examples of specific founders and their views. And so, he cites the adoption of the Northwest Ordinance by the Articles of Confederation Congress; the act of the first Congress under the Constitution to enforce the Northwest Ordinance; and the fact that this act was signed by George Washington. He refers to Congress's organization of the Southwest Territory—what became Tennessee, Mississippi, and Alabama—where Congress didn't prohibit slavery, but did regulate it. He talks about the prohibition on importing slaves into the Louisiana Territory. He talks about the Missouri Compromise. All of these things illustrate Congressional regulation of slavery, which Douglas said the founding fathers opposed. Lincoln marshals all these different kinds of evidence to add up a number of the founding fathers, and to conclude that a majority of the signers of the Constitution believed that Congress had the power to regulate slavery, which was the position opposite to Douglas's, and opposite to Douglas's use of the founding fathers. It's a remarkable speech, both for the specificity and the range of evidence that Lincoln uses.

I think we can get a better appreciation for what Lincoln did if we take some time to explore the different types of evidence. While different theorists categorize evidence different ways, I'm going to group evidence under the headings of examples, statistics, tangible objects, testimony, and social consensus; so we'll have five main categories of evidence.

I begin with examples. These could include a brief mention of an instance without any development of it. It's become common in the years since President Reagan for the president of the United States, when he delivers the State of the Union address, to have sitting in the First Lady's box one or more special guests who will be briefly mentioned during the speech as an example of some quality or other that the president wishes to praise. Nothing is said in any detail about these people. They are recognized, asked to stand and to receive applause, and they're cited as an example. It's a very brief mention.

Or take an example that could be developed more elaborately as an illustration of some point or other: famously, during the 2000 presidential debates, then Vice President Al Gore spoke at some length about conditions in a school in Florida that was overcrowded, that a student had to stand up; there weren't enough desks, and supplies, and so on, available. It turned out that Vice President Gore was not entirely correct about his facts, but what he was doing was offering an illustration, an extended example. In either case, whether it's a brief mention or an extended example, what the arguer is doing is providing the materials from which he or she will build a generalization, to say that something is true about a category as a whole.

One can argue about whether or not the examples support the generalization, and we'll see in the very next lecture, in fact, how we do that; but the truth of the examples themselves has to be accepted before that argument can take place. If the examples are not considered true, then we have to have a separate argument to bear out their truth for them to be able to serve as evidence. Examples are one very common type of evidence.

Another type of evidence we see quite often is statistics. There are all sorts of kinds of statistics, and if this were a course on statistics we'd cover them in much more detail; but let me just highlight some of the different ways that statistics can serve as evidence. The simplest statistics are raw numbers. There have been two father-son pairs of U.S. presidents as of 2005, for example. Or, over 1,700 U.S. soldiers died in Iraq as of mid-2005. Raw numbers that nothing has been done to are the simplest kind of statistic.

Percentages, ratios, and index numbers are statistics that have been refined a bit by analysis. For example, 55 percent of baby boomers are planning to retire before they reach the normal retirement age; this is a percentage. The ratio of women to men in nursing schools is 8:1—a ratio that tells us, for every one of one category we have eight of another. Or if the price of gasoline in 1993 was 100, it would be 240 now—that's an index where numbers are placed against a standard, which is usually set to be 100. What those all do beyond simply reporting raw numbers is to give the numbers some meaning by putting them in context. A percentage says that out of 100 we have this; a ratio says, here's how the categories compare; and so on.

Other kinds of statistics include the measures of central tendency, of which the famous ones are the mean, the median, and the mode. Let's say the average price of a new home is $425,000. If we mean by that the mean price, we would take all the homes in the country in that were sold, add up the sale prices, divide them by the number of homes, and we'd get that number $425,000. If we said $425,000 was the median, we mean that it's the one middle— half of the homes sold cost more, half of the homes sold cost less. If we say it's the modal price, we mean it's the most often cited price—so more homes were sold for $425,000 than for any other price.

Another kind of statistical measure is the rate of change. For example, the city of Las Vegas is gaining 20,000 new people per day; that's a rate of change. Or probability statements, including the outcomes of controlled experiments and studies: these results are significant at the .05 level, meaning that if we did this experiment over and over again, 95 percent of the time we would not get this result just by chance.

Each one of these statistical forms is subject to tests for its accuracy. In order for statistics to function as evidence, the truth of the statistics must be accepted. Of course, it's an old adage that you can prove anything you want to with statistics, depending upon how you contextualize the statistics and what statistics you use. Their accuracy needs to be established for the purposes of their serving as evidence in an argument. In sum, we have examples and we have statistics as types of evidence.

Another form of evidence is tangible objects: actual things or pictures of the actual things. These figure prominently as evidence in criminal law. For example, it's very important in a murder trial to be able to find the murder weapon. If the murder weapon can't be discovered, then there's an important piece that's missing in the chain of evidence that has to be established in order to make a case for a conviction. For example, in the mid-1990s in the O.J. Simpson murder trial, one key question was regarding a glove found on the scene. Did it fit Mr. Simpson or not? The glove was a tangible object that functioned as evidence to support or to oppose the claim that O.J. Simpson likely committed the act for which he had been charged.

Sometimes the tangible object is important historically, as in the discovery of particular artifacts, and they need not be ancient artifacts. In the 1940s in the Alger Hiss case, the case that made Richard Nixon famous, the case turned on the existence of some microfilm papers. The microfilms were found in a hollowed-out pumpkin on a farm in Maryland, right where a key witness had said they would be. The availability of those microfilms was very important as a tangible object.

The significance of tangible objects is properly captured in the adage, "a picture is worth a thousand words." This may be why, to refer back to Colin Powell's speech before the UN Security Council, Secretary Powell showed so many photographs and videos as part of his presentation; and at one point, in a now controversial move, held up a vial, which he claimed represented the uranium that Iraq was trying to obtain in Africa. Sometimes, however, even words will be tangible objects, as in the example of a historical document. The U.S. Constitution could be cited as a specific document; or legal contracts could be cited; or any kind of agreement; or letters; or diaries. These are tangible objects that exist in documentary form.

So far, then, we have examples, statistics, and tangible objects. In each case, the truth of the evidence has to be accepted in order for the argument to proceed. When I mentioned Lincoln at Cooper Union, I hope you can see already how Lincoln used several different kinds of evidence. He used examples: he counted up the number of founders, a simple case of statistics. And, he used tangible objects: he used documents.

Another kind of evidence, the fourth kind I want to mention, is testimony of fact or of opinion. We rely on testimony a lot because there are lots of things that for each of us we can't know directly. We're not qualified to have a reliable opinion. And so we rely on the judgment of people who are in a position to know directly and who do have a reliable opinion. We accept testimony because of the credibility of the source.

Aristotle wrote about what he called *ethos*, by which he meant "the apparent character of a person"—not necessarily the person's real true inner character, but the judgments that someone else makes about the character of the person. If you judge me to be a trustworthy person, whether I am or not, then my *ethos* is positive as far as you're concerned; you've made a positive judgment about my character.

Ethos, or credibility, has been shown through research to be composed of judgments about the following traits: competence—do I know what I'm talking about; trustworthiness, or goodwill—am I positively disposed toward you; and dynamism—do I seem to be energetic in what I'm saying? Those are all factors that will lead people to judge me as being a credible source.

Credibility can be established either for one's self, or one could derive credibility by using credible sources. For instance, eyewitness access to information will make one a credible source in a courtroom. If I saw it happen, I'll be more credible than if I didn't. Background and training will make one a credible source. For example, every four years, when there are presidential debates, I get called up by the news media for my opinion, and I enjoy my 15 minutes of fame. Why do I get called? Because somebody believes that I have background and expertise in the evaluations of arguments that would be pertinent to the presidential debates. A good track record will make a person a credible source. For instance, for much of the 1990s and into the early 2000s, Alan Greenspan was regarded as a credible source on what the Federal Reserve was up to and what the economy would do, because for a long period of time he had a good track record of calling things right and making good judgments. All of these things will make a person perceived to be a more credible source. And so, I can rely on my own credibility, or I can cite sources that have been established to be credible, in offering testimony.

We have to be careful though, because there also are factors that could call a person's credibility or ethos into doubt, and would then require a separate argument to establish the evidence. For instance, is the person an authority on the subject about which he or she speaks? Entertainment and sports celebrities often speak out, for example, on political questions for which they may not have any expertise or any special authority. Is there a clear basis on which the person reached the conclusion, or is he or she just mouthing off a personal preference without anything to back it up? Does the person have a bias or vested interest? Is there a reason for the person to express a particular opinion, because it will benefit him or her to do that? We call that eager evidence, if a person stands to gain for something he or she says. And if the person stands to lose by making a statement, and makes the statement anyway, we call that reluctant evidence, and regard it as more credible because it's in opposition to the person's own self interest. A final question to ask is, do credible sources disagree? Is the person whose testimony is being quoted representative, or is he or she the outlier among equally credible sources? We want to be sure that we have a credible source, because testimony relies on the credibility of the source. If we're not sure, then we raise these tests, and we have another argument to establish credibility, in order that it may serve as evidence.

Those are four of the categories of evidence. The remaining one I have called social consensus, and by that I mean things that are so generally believed that an audience treats them as if they were facts. They're just good as facts for that particular audience. Even though the beliefs may turn out later not have been well-founded, at the time, they function as if they were facts.

For instance, common knowledge is a type of social consensus—things that everybody believes to be true. In the late 1990s and early 2000s, the belief that politicians manipulate budget numbers could be called a piece of common knowledge. All of the disputes about the budget deficit, and then budget surplus, and then the budget deficit again—which was real? What should be done with them? It was commonly accepted that these numbers were manipulated to serve political purposes. Another kind of social consensus are shared value judgments. Most people and certainly most critical audiences would place a high priority on what would be good for children, particularly their own children. What would benefit the next generation? We find public figures of all political persuasions claiming that what they want is, in a famous slogan, "to leave no child behind," and to emphasize a priority for children. Valuing children is a kind of social consensus.

Shared historical understandings are another type of social consensus. For example, in the United States, it is widely believed that the United States won the cold war by the late 1980s. It is widely believed that the Civil Rights Movement made great gains during the 1960s, and these widely shared historical understandings focus a kind of social consensus. Conclusions that have been established already in an argument can be considered an item of social consensus, and they can be used as if they were facts because the audience has already agreed to them; they've already been established as a result of a previous argument. Then finally, in the particular discussion, things can be stipulated when we say, "Let's assume for the sake of argument." The phrase "for the sake of argument" is saying, we're going to stipulate for this particular discussion that something or other is true; and then in this discussion, it will function as an example of social consensus. If there are differences in core values or common knowledge, they'll need to be resolved before social consensus can be accepted as evidence.

I want to clue you in on one thing. I've said in all of these examples of what counts as evidence that our standard is what a critical audience would accept. That's a good normative standard, but we should note that actual audiences often have looser standards. Judgments of the quality of the evidence are affected by whether one agrees with the claim. They're affected by a speaker's delivery. They're affected by whether the source is familiar. Evidence is most influential when an audience is unfamiliar with the subject matter, and when the goal is sustained attitude change over time. What do we make of the fact that there's a discrepancy between what people accept as evidence and the standards that we suggest? It doesn't mean we should abandon our standards because we want to improve the quality of argument. When we examine arguments and when we construct them, we'll try to reach a higher standard.

We've talked now about claims and about evidence. In the next lecture we'll begin to talk about inferences and warrants.

Glossary

A fortiori: argument suggesting that what is true of the lesser is true of the greater, or vice versa.

Ad hominem: argument against the person; usually regarded as a fallacy if it replaces substantive argument with personal attack but sometimes an appropriate criticism of another person's character, bias, or inconsistency.

Ambiguity: a condition in which a word could be used with multiple meanings and it is not clear from the context of the argument which meaning is intended.

Amphiboly: a condition in which a phrase or clause could be used with multiple meanings and it is not clear from the context of the argument which meaning is intended.

Amplitude: the number and range of arguments assembled to support a claim; the greater the number and diversity of arguments, the greater the amplitude.

Analogy: an inference based on resemblances: things that are alike in most respects are probably alike in the respect in question.

Antecedent: the "if" clause in an "if-then" conditional statement.

Bandwagon effect: accepting or rejecting a claim not on the basis of its merits but simply on the basis that many others are doing so.

Begging the question: assuming in an argument something that actually requires proof.

Burden of proof: the ultimate responsibility to demonstrate that a claim or resolution is probably true.

Burden of rejoinder: the responsibility to continue the argument after a plausible initial case has been made for or against the resolution.

Case: the structure of arguments developed to support or to oppose the resolution.

Categorical: a form of the syllogism in which statements relate categories to other categories; the relation is either inclusion or exclusion.

Cause: an inference that one factor somehow exerts influence on another; the inference not only asserts a predictable relationship between the factors but also accounts for it.

Circular reasoning: repeating in the claim what is already stated in the evidence, with the result that there is no inference or progression in the argument.

Claim: the statement of fact, definition, value, or policy that an arguer asks the audience to accept.

Classification: reasoning by example, in which the move is from a general statement to a specific claim.

Coalescent argumentation: argumentation in which the goal is to maximize the interests of both parties rather than to produce a winner and a loser.

Commonplaces: general beliefs or values that are widely shared within a culture.

Composition, fallacy of: the assumption that what is true of each of the parts is necessarily true of the whole.

Condensation symbols: symbols, such as a national flag, that embody (or "condense") a wide range of emotions or connotations; people will share a positive or negative reaction to the symbol although they will have very different reasons for doing so.

Conditional: a form of the syllogism that begins with an "if-then" statement, either affirms or denies the "if" or the "then" clause, and reaches some conclusion about the other clause.

Consequent: the "then" clause in an "if-then" conditional statement.

Controversy: a genuine disagreement between people that matters to them and that they wish to resolve.

Convergent: an organizational pattern in which a group of independent claims, taken together, supports the resolution or in which a group of independent pieces of evidence, taken together, support the claim.

Correlation: a measure of the predictable relationship between two factors, of the degree to which the presence of one predicts the presence of the other, or to which change in one predicts change in the other.

Credibility: the believability of a source; the product of competence, trustworthiness, good will, and dynamism as these are understood by the audience.

Critical discussion: an interpersonal argument in which both parties want to resolve rather than merely settle the dispute, each has an equal opportunity to influence the other, both want to resolve the dispute on the merits rather than by reference to extraneous factors, and there are no artificial constraints on their ability to resolve the dispute.

Deduction: reasoning in which the claim follows necessarily and automatically from the evidence and contains no new information not present at least implicitly in the evidence.

Dialectic: a process of discovering and testing knowledge through questions and answers.

Dilemma: an argument in which one presumably is confronted with an exhaustive set of possibilities, all of which are undesirable yet one of which must be selected.

Disjunctive: form of the syllogism that begins with an "either-or" statement, affirms or denies one of the options, and makes a claim about the other.

Dissociation: the breaking of a previously unitary term or concept into two separate ideas, one of which is more positively valued than the other, then identifying one's own argument with the more positively valued term.

Distribution: a property of terms in a categorical syllogism; a term is distributed if the statement containing it refers to every member of the category that the term designates.

Division, fallacy of: the assumption that what is true of the whole is necessarily true of each of the parts.

End terms: the terms in a categorical syllogism that appear in one premise as well as in the conclusion.

Enthymeme: a structure of reasoning in which one or more of the premises is drawn (often implicitly) from the beliefs of a particular audience; the argument is valid for that specific audience; sometimes described as a rhetorical syllogism.

Equivocation: the shifting of the meaning or sense of a term in the course of the argument.

Essentially contested concepts: concepts that gain their meaning or significance only in opposition to other concepts.

Evidence: statements that are offered in support of a claim.

Example: an inference that relates parts and wholes: that what is true of one is probably true of the other; *also* a type of evidence that consists of specific instances of a more general claim.

Fallacy: conventionally understood as an argument that appears to be valid but is not; sometimes used loosely to refer to any deficiency in an argument; more specifically, identifies deficiencies in form or (according to some theorists) in procedure.

False dilemma: a purported dilemma in which the alternatives are not exhaustive (there are other unmentioned possibilities) or in which they are not all undesirable.

Figurative analogy: an analogy that asserts a similarity in the relationships among things, events, places, and so on, rather than among the items themselves.

Formal reasoning: reasoning in which claims follow from evidence purely as a matter of form, so that content and context are irrelevant; often equated with deduction, mathematical reasoning, and/or symbolic logic.

Generalization: inference from example in which the movement is from specific evidence to a general claim.

Hasty generalization: a generalization made on the basis of an insufficient number of examples.

Heap: the argument that, because each increment of something will be of no consequence, no amount of increment can be of consequence and a "critical mass" cannot be achieved.

Induction: reasoning in which the claim follows from the evidence only with some degree of probability and in which the claim contains new information not present in the evidence.

Inference: a mental move from evidence to a claim so that one accepts the claim on the basis of the evidence.

Informal reasoning: reasoning that is not purely a matter of form; in which content and context cannot be ignored.

Issue: a question that is inherent in the resolution and vital to its success; an argument that must be established in order to establish the claim contained in the resolution.

Literal analogy: an analogy that is a direct comparison of objects, events, places, and so on, starting with the knowledge that they are basically alike and inferring that they are probably alike in the respect under consideration.

Logic: structures of reasoning, whether formal or informal; the concern is with the relationships among statements rather than the relationships between statements and audiences.

Middle term: the term in a categorical syllogism that appears in the premises but not in the conclusion.

Mini-max principle: a guideline for strategic choices in attack and defense: one should make those choices that, with minimum effort and risk, yield the maximum gain.

Mixed controversy: a controversy in which the participants are committed to defending opposing claims and in which, therefore, each participant assumes a burden of proof.

Multiple controversy: a controversy in which more than one claim is advanced at the same time.

Narrative: an inference from the coherence of elements in a story or plot line.

Non sequitur: an argument in which the claim has no conceivable relationship to the evidence and does not follow from it.

Objective data: evidence that can be independently established or verified and to which it is widely agreed.

Parallel: an organizational structure in which each claim independently establishes the resolution, or each piece of evidence independently establishes the claim.

Personal sphere: the sphere of argument in which disputes concern only the participants and are resolved by them; typically, argumentation is private and ephemeral.

Persuasive definition: a definition that changes the denotation of a term while retaining the positive or negative connotation.

Phoros: the pair of terms in a figurative analogy that is better known; the relationship between them will be used to infer a similar relationship between the other two terms.

***Post hoc* fallacy**: the assumption that because one event followed another, the first somehow caused the second.

Presence: salience, importance, conscious awareness.

Presumption: a descriptive characteristic of the position that would prevail in the absence of argumentation; the arguer who does not hold presumption must present a case sufficiently compelling to outweigh it.

Prima facie: literally, "at first face"; a case that, on the surface, seems to satisfy the burden of proof unless something is said against it.

Proof: support for a claim; reasons to justify acceptance of a claim; not to be confused with scientific demonstration or mathematical certainty.

Public sphere: the sphere of argument that is of general interest to people in their capacity as citizens and in which everyone is eligible to participate.

Red herring: irrelevant material that may be introduced into an argument to distract or to deflect attention.

Reductio ad absurdum: method of refutation that suggests the other arguer's position leads to unacceptable implications.

Refutation: the process of criticizing, attacking, or responding to an argument; sometimes the term is also used to embrace the process of defending, rebuilding, or extending an argument after it has been attacked or criticized.

Resolution: the ultimate claim that an advocate seeks to prove or disprove; the substance of a controversy; a declarative statement that responds to the central question in a controversy.

Rhetoric: study of the ways messages influence people; the faculty of discovering the available means of persuasion in a given case.

Self-sealing: an argument that cannot be tested or falsified because its warrant accounts for all possibilities, even those that seemingly would disconfirm the claim.

Series: an organizational structure in which each claim or piece of evidence leads to the next, only at the end of the chain leading to the resolution or claim in question.

Sign: an inference from the predictable relationship between factors; the presence of one predicts the presence of the other; or change in one predicts change in the other.

Single controversy: a controversy in which only one claim is involved; the claim is advanced by one participant and doubted by the other.

Slippery slope: an argument that suggests that a seemingly trivial or inconsequential action will start an irreversible chain of events leading to catastrophe.

Social knowledge: the conventional wisdom or common judgment of a society that is accepted and acted on as true.

Sphere: a metaphorical arena for argumentation in which a distinctive set of accumulated expectations defines the context and the range of persons eligible to participate.

Stasis: the focal point of a controversy; the question on which the controversy turns; the "point of rest" at which the force of an assertion is countered by the force of a denial.

Straw man: an answer to an argument that has not been advanced and that is not germane to the matter under discussion.

Syllogism: a standard structure of reasoning that contains two premises and a conclusion; the premises are the evidence, and the conclusion is the claim; the conclusion is derived from the premises.

Technical sphere: the sphere of argument in which controversy takes place in specialized fields, is governed by the conventions of the field, and is accessible to people in the field.

Theme: the pair of terms in a figurative analogy about which the conclusion will be drawn; the relationship between the terms in the other, well-known pair will be used to infer a relationship between the terms in this pair.

Topoi: literally, "places"; categories of issues that typically arise in resolutions of a given type.

Unmixed controversy: a controversy in which only one participant commits to defending a claim and assuming a burden of proof; the other party casts doubt on that claim but does not advance a competing claim.

Vagueness: the property of a term that is of indeterminate meaning or that has multiple meanings, but the meaning intended in the case at hand cannot be determined.

Validity: in formal reasoning, a condition in which, if the evidence is true, the claim must be true (to have true evidence and a false claim would be contradictory); in informal reasoning, a content-neutral test of the soundness or compelling nature of a claim.

Warrant: an authorization or license to make the inference from evidence to claim.

Biographical Notes

Aristotle (384–322 B.C.E.) Wrote a systematic treatise on the art of rhetoric, which he defined as the faculty of discovering the available means of persuasion in a given case. Identified forms of argument and genres of appeal.

Descartes, Renè (1596–1650). Philosopher who used systematic doubt to find the basis of knowledge in self-evident statements. Cartesian logic regards only formal deduction as acceptable reasoning.

Eemeren, Frans H. van. (1946–). Professor of argumentation studies at the University of Amsterdam. One of the founders and principal proponents of the pragma-dialectical approach to argument analysis.

Farrell, Thomas B. (1947–). Professor of Communication Studies, Northwestern University. Rhetorical critic and theorist of the public sphere; contemporary interpreter of Aristotle. Introduced the concept of *social knowledge* to designate a community's storehouse of conventional wisdom that is accepted as true.

Goodnight, G. Thomas (1948–). Professor of Communication in the Annenberg School for Communication, University of Southern California. Postulated controversy as the basic defining unit of argumentation; described the liberal and the conservative presumptions in argument; distinguished among the personal, technical, and public spheres of argument.

Gorgias (c. A.D. 483–c. 376 B.C.E.). Sophist who developed and taught figures of speech and stylistic variation, although not in a systematic fashion.

Grice, H. P. (1915–1988). A philosopher of language who analyzed ordinary conversations and developed normative principles for language use that are implicitly understood by the participants in a successful exchange.

Grootendorst, Rob (1943–2000). Professor of argumentation studies at the University of Amsterdam; one of the co-developers of the pragma-dialectical approach to argumentation studies.

Habermas, Jürgen (1929–). German social theorist who has described the transformation of the public sphere from its 18th-century ideal to an increasingly bureaucratized and technical forum.

Hamblin, C. L. (1922–1985). Australian philosopher who challenged conventional views of fallacies by suggesting that they should be seen as units of discourse that were not fallacious in all circumstances.

Isocrates (436–338 B.C.E.). A Sophist who taught by modeling examples of outstanding practice rather than by formal precept; a leading antagonist of Plato.

Lippmann, Walter (1889–1974). Journalist, theorist, and critic of politics and society. Argued in the 1920s that the public was not competent to make judgments about policy; qualified this view during the 1950s by maintaining that it was possible to cultivate a "public philosophy."

Mill, John Stuart (1806–1873). English utilitarian philosopher; developed systems for inferring causation that are the basis for most social science research.

O'Keefe, Daniel J. (1950–). Professor of Communication Studies, Northwestern University. Called attention to two separate perspectives on argumentation, as both product (text) and process (interaction) with different methods and objectives of study for each.

Peirce, Charles Sanders (1839–1914). American pragmatist philosopher who maintained that there were four principal ways of knowing: tenacity, authority, correspondence with *a priori* beliefs, and verification (the scientific method).

Perelman, Chaim (1922–1984). Belgian philosopher of jurisprudence; together with Mme. L. Olbrechts-Tyteca, developed a system of rhetoric in which argument is the fundamental unit; introduced such concepts as presence, dissociation, and the universal audience.

Plato (c. 428–347 B.C.E.). Philosopher who attacked the Sophists and assumed that their excesses were inherent in their practice; distinguished rhetoric (concerned with appearances) from philosophy (concerned with truth).

Protagoras (c. 445 B.C.E.). Sophist who often is regarded as the "father of debate" because he taught that every question has two sides and that "man is the measure of all things."

Ramus, Peter (1515–1572). Dutch philosopher who refigured the relationship between philosophy and rhetoric by regarding invention and arrangement as part of philosophy and logic, leaving rhetoric with only style and delivery.

Stevenson, Charles L. (1908–1979). Philosopher of language who introduced the concept of the persuasive definition, which transfers positive or negative connotation from one denotation to another.

Toulmin, Stephen (1922–). British philosopher who has held several academic appointments in the United States; theorized that formal logic is an inappropriate prototype for argumentation and developed a model of argument as an alternative to the syllogism.

Walton, Douglas N. (1942–). Professor of Philosophy at the University of Winnipeg. Engaged in a systematic study of the fallacies to determine more precisely the conditions under which they may be valid arguments.

Whately, Richard (1787–1863). Archbishop of Dublin; developed a theory of presumption that he applied to every existing institution on the grounds that change is not a good in itself.

Willard, Charles Arthur (1945–). Leading proponent of the view that argumentation should be seen primarily as a type of interaction in which persons maintain what they construe to be incompatible positions; has written extensively on argument fields and the need for interfield borrowing of discourse.

Bibliography

Benoit, William L., Dale Hample, and Pamela J. Benoit, eds. *Readings in Argumentation.* Berlin: Foris, 1992. An anthology containing more than 35 articles, originally published in scholarly journals, on different areas of argumentation.

Braet, Antoine. "The Classical Doctrine of *Status* and the Rhetorical Theory of Argumentation," *Philosophy and Rhetoric* 20 (1987), 79–93. Relates the legal concept of *stasis* (or, in Latin, *status*) to argumentation theory.

Corbett, Edward P. J., and Rosa A. Eberly. *The Elements of Reasoning*, 2nd ed. Boston: Allyn and Bacon, 2000. A basic introduction to reasoning based on the concept of *stasis*.

Cox, J. Robert, and Charles Arthur Willard, eds. *Advances in Argumentation Theory and Research.* Carbondale: Southern Illinois University Press, 1982. An anthology of original essays commissioned to celebrate the 30th anniversary of the American Forensic Association.

Eemeren, Frans H. van, Rob Grootendorst, Sally Jackson, and Scott Jacobs. *Reconstructing Argumentative Discourse.* Tuscaloosa: University of Alabama Press, 1993. Integrates the pragma-dialectical approach of van Eemeren and Grootendorst with the discourse-analysis approach of Jackson and Jacobs to study naturally occurring arguments in interpersonal settings.

Eemeren, Frans H. van, Rob Grootendorst, and Francisca Snoeck Henkemans. *Argumentation: Analysis, Evaluation, Presentation.* Mahwah, N.J.: Erlbaum, 2002. Accessible textbook that develops a pragma-dialectical approach to argumentation; includes discussion of fallacies as procedural errors.

Eemeren, Frans H. van,, Rob Grootendorst, Francisca Snoeck Henkemans, J. Anthony Blair, Ralph H. Johnson, Erik C. W. Crabbe, Christian Plantin, Douglas N. Walton, Charles A. Willard, John Woods, and David Zarefsky. *Fundamentals of Argumentation Theory: A Handbook of Historical Backgrounds and Contemporary Developments.* Mahwah, N.J.: Erlbaum, 1996. Overview essays describing the state of the art in argumentation theory from different perspectives represented in European and North American scholarship.

Farrell, Thomas B. "Knowledge, Consensus, and Rhetorical Theory." *Quarterly Journal of Speech* 62 (February 1976), 1–14. Explains the concept of *social knowledge* and explores how it functions in public discourse.

———. *Norms of Rhetorical Culture.* New Haven: Yale University Press, 1993. Develops a theory of society and culture grounded in respect for the practice of argumentation and rhetoric.

Fogelin, Robert J., and Walter Sinnott-Armstrong. *Understanding Arguments: An Introduction to Informal Logic,* 5th ed. Fort Worth: Harcourt Brace, 1997. Sophisticated presentation of the basic reasoning patterns of formal and informal logic and a discussion of their differences.

Freeley, Austin J., and David L. Steinberg. *Argumentation and Debate: Critical Thinking for Reasoned Decision Making,* 10th ed. Belmont, Calif.: Wadsworth, 2000. The leading textbook in argumentation and debate.

Gilbert, Michael A. *Coalescent Argumentation.* Mahwah, N.J.: Erlbaum, 1997. Develops a theory of argumentation in interpersonal encounters as multi-modal and fundamentally cooperative.

Gottlieb, Gidon. *The Logic of Choice: An Investigation of the Concepts of Rule and Rationality.* London: Allen and Unwin, 1968. Develops a theory of the significance of reasoning with rules, especially in law.

Gross, Alan G., and Ray D. Dearin. *Chaim Perelman.* Albany: State University of New York Press, 2003. An exposition of Perelman's basic theories of argument with examples that will be meaningful to a U.S. audience.

Habermas, Jürgen. *Structural Transformation of the Public Sphere.* Cambridge, Mass.: MIT Press, 1989 (1962). Develops a theory of the weakening of the public sphere during the 20th century.

Hauser, Gerard A. *Vernacular Voices: The Rhetoric of Publics and Public Spheres.* Columbia, S.C.: University of South Carolina Press, 1999. Argues that multiple publics can be discerned by attending to the arguments and rhetorical style of ordinary citizens.

Herrick, James A. *Argumentation: Understanding and Shaping Arguments.* State College, Penna: Strata Publishing, 2004. A highly accessible argumentation textbook, which focuses especially on argument schemes (patterns of warrants and inferences).

Johnson, Ralph H. *Manifest Rationality: A Pragmatic Theory of Argument.* Mahwah, N.J.: Erlbaum 2000. Assesses the state of argumentation theory, primarily from the perspective of informal logic, and offers the construct of "manifest rationality" as a way to fill gaps in existing theory.

Johnstone, Henry W., Jr. *The Problem of the Self.* University Park: Pennsylvania State University Press, 1970. Suggests that the self is discovered only through one's willingness to risk it by engaging in critical argumentation.

Kuhn, Thomas S. *The Structure of Scientific Revolutions,* 2nd ed. Chicago: University of Chicago Press, 1970. Distinguishes between normal and revolutionary science and maintains that discourse in the latter takes place outside the conventions of seemingly deductive normal science.

Levi, Edward H. *An Introduction to Legal Reasoning.* Chicago: University of Chicago Press, 1949. A standard introductory volume on the nature of legal reasoning, embracing neither the ideal of formal deduction nor the contemporary critical view that law is primarily a cloak for power.

Lunsford, Andrea A., John J. Ruszkiewicz, and Keith Walters, eds. *Everything's an Argument,* 3rd ed. Discussion of argumentation principles and theories with special attention to the writing classroom.

Nadeau, Ray. "Hermogenes' *On Stases:* A Translation with an Introduction and Notes," *Communication Monographs* 31 (November 1964), 361–424. Makes available in English the leading classical writing on the subject of *stasis.*

Newman, Robert P., and Dale R. Newman. *Evidence.* Boston: Houghton Mifflin, 1969. A thorough treatment of different types of evidence and tests for evaluating evidence.

Parry-Giles, Trevor, and Shawn J. Parry-Giles. "Reassessing the State of Political Communication in the United States," *Argumentation and Advocacy* 37 (Winter 2001), 148–170. Challenges the widespread belief that the quality of American political discourse has declined during the contemporary period.

Patterson, J. W., and David Zarefsky. *Contemporary Debate.* Boston: Houghton Mifflin, 1983. Grounds its analysis of debate in the general study of argumentation, which is seen as a means to test hypotheses for their probable truth.

Perelman, Chaim. *The Realm of Rhetoric,* translated by William Kluback. Notre Dame: University of Notre Dame Press, 1982. A briefer version of the author's theory of argument developed more fully in *The New Rhetoric* (1969 [1958]).

Rieke, Richard D., and Malcolm O. Sillars. *Argumentation and Critical Decision Making,* 4th ed. New York: Longman, 1997. A leading textbook in general argumentation; relates theories and principles to the study of specific fields.

Sloane, Thomas O., ed. *Encyclopedia of Rhetoric.* New York: Oxford University Press, 2001. Contains article-length entries on major topics in argumentation and rhetorical theory, including brief biographies.

Stevenson, Charles L. *Ethics in Language.* New Haven: Yale University Press, 1944. Formulates the idea of *persuasive definition* and theorizes how it works.

Thomas, David A., and Jack P. Hart, eds. *Advanced Debate: Readings in Theory, Practice, and Teaching,* 4th ed. Lincolnwood, Ill.: National Textbook, 1992. An anthology of articles about argumentation and debate theory and practice that originally appeared in scholarly journals.

Toulmin, Stephen. *The Uses of Argument.* Cambridge: Cambridge University Press, 1958. A now-classic work in which the author indicts formal argument as a prototype and proposes an alternative scheme represented in a diagram known as the Toulmin model.

Trapp, Robert, and Janice Schuetz, eds. *Perspectives on Argumentation: Essays in Honor of Wayne Brockriede.* Prospect Heights, Ill.: Waveland Press, 1990. An anthology of original essays exploring different approaches to the study and practice of argumentation.

Walton, Douglas. *Ad Hominem Arguments.* Tuscaloosa: University of Alabama Press, 1998. Distinguishes among various types of *ad hominem* arguments and considers conditions under which the argument is and is not fallacious.

———. "Persuasive Definitions and Public Policy Arguments," *Argumentation and Advocacy* 37 (Winter 2001), 117–132. Examines the role of definitional strategies in a variety of political arguments.

———. *A Pragmatic Theory of Fallacy.* Tuscaloosa: University of Alabama Press, 1995. Challenges the conventional view that fallacies are violations of form and suggests instead that they should be understood as violations of dialogue procedure.

Willard, Charles Arthur. *A Theory of Argumentation.* Tuscaloosa: University of Alabama Press, 1989. The most complete statement of Willard's view that argumentation should be seen primarily as a type of communicative interaction.

Zarefsky, David. *Public Speaking: Strategies for Success*, 4th ed. Boston: Allyn and Bacon, 2005. A textbook treatment of public speaking that draws heavily on concepts in argumentation theory and practice.